APPETIZERS AT DEVON

A Collection of Recipes
from the Devon Horse Show
and Country Fair

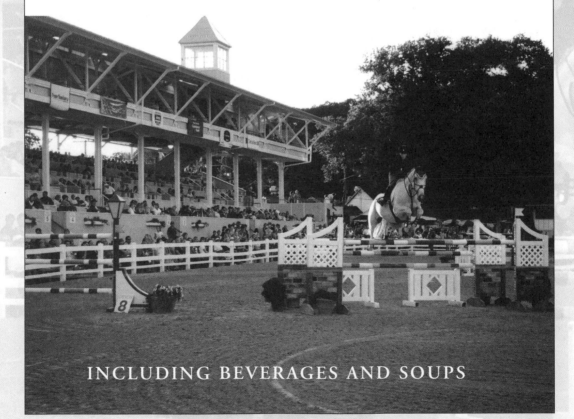

INCLUDING BEVERAGES AND SOUPS

APPETIZERS AT DEVON

A Collection of Recipes from the Devon Horse Show and Country Fair

Published by the Devon Horse Show and Country Fair
Copyright © 2008 by
Devon Horse Show and Country Fair
P.O. Box 865
Devon, Pennsylvania 19333
610-964-0550

Cover photography © by Brenda Carpenter
Artwork © by Helena Van Emmerick-Finn

This cookbook is a collection of our favorite recipes,
which are not necessarily original recipes.

ISBN: 978-0-9798665-0-0

Edited, Designed, and Manufactured by
CommunityClassics™

An imprint of

FRP.

P.O. Box 305142
Nashville, Tennessee 37230
800-358-0560

Manufactured in China
First Printing 2008
10,000 copies

 denotes classic Devon recipes

INVESTING IN OUR FUTURE

We believe that gifts to the Devon Horse Show and Country Fair are much more than an investment in property and buildings or an act of support for the national and international equestrian community. More importantly, each gift is an investment in our community's future and the quality of life we are blessed with here on the Philadelphia Main Line and beyond.

The Devon Horse Show and Country Fair stands apart as one of the nation's oldest and most prestigious outdoor horse shows. Started in 1896, Devon has grown from a one-day event to an eleven-day spectacle, drawing competitors and spectators from around the world.

With attendance exceeding 100,000 each May, the Devon Horse Show and Country Fair serves as a boom to the local economy, generating approximately $5 million in revenue each year for area hotels, restaurants, and shops over the eleven-day period. The other shows held on the grounds generate another $5 million annually.

Proceeds from the event, as they have since 1919, benefit Bryn Mawr Hospital with its long-standing mission, "to heal the sick, comfort the suffering, and conserve the life of the community." Devon has contributed more than $10 million to the hospital over the years.

The Devon Horse Show and Country Fair brings together three thousand volunteers from all walks of life who work year-round in support of the show. Clearly, this is a tangible sign of the pride area residents have in both the show and the hospital and a worthy outlet for the eager to give back to their community.

The Devon Horse Show
A History

*Delicacies and Devon have been inexorably entwined
since the very beginning.*

1896

*At first, it was high tea served on the front porch of the Devon Inn so guests
could watch the Horse Show being held on the front lawn. Other spectators, a
colorful mixture of farmers, horse breeders and horsemen, would bring sandwiches
tied up in brown paper and provide their own chairs to sit around the ring.*

1910

*Sandwiches and brown paper gave way to picnic hampers after the turn of the
century, while the hodgepodge of chairs gave way to polished automobiles and
hansom carriages parked around the ring. Those spectators arriving by the
Pennsylvania Railroad could eat their picnics in the new wooden grandstand
with forty-six boxes protected by a canvas awning.*

1919

*After the First World War, the first food was donated for sale at a booth with the
proceeds going to Byrn Mawr Hospital. The food booth was a great success with
delighted horse show patrons. The following year, culinary delights prepared by
private cooks employed in mansions across the Main Line were donated to the cause
and delivered to the food booth by liveried chauffeurs wearing puttees. The same
year, 1920, William DuPont, Jr., built the first stables on the property.*

1941

Just prior to America's involvement in the Second World War, the first lighted ring and evening classes were added to the show. Now patrons could have dinner at Devon as well. The grandstands with private boxes became the place to tear pheasant while watching one's favorite jumping classes. With the end of the prohibition, adult beverages became part of the evening ritual as well. By now there were enough stables to house nearly three hundred horses.

1950–1990

The four decades following the Second World War brought change and growth to Devon. The food offerings at the Country Fair were so varied and delicious that fewer patrons lugged hampers to the grounds. Additional stabling was built so the show could accommodate nearly 900 horses, and new grandstands were built with the number of private boxes rising to 333 (including 24 sky boxes). Through it all, young ladies carried wicker trays up and down the grandstands selling lemon sticks (a lemon pierced with a candy stick), a tradition that goes on even today.

Another Century

With the millennium celebrations in 2000, Devon found itself operating in a third century, as 2006 marked our 110th anniversary year. Instead of donating delicacies from our kitchens for sale at the Country Fair, we hope that this book raises the monies needed to restore the stables that first appeared at the same time the food booths did at Devon. Delicacies and Devon... Still inexorably entwined.

Samuel W. W. Griffin

Proceeds from the sale of this cookbook
will go toward the restoration of the historic barns
on the Devon Horse Show grounds.

Contents

Definition of Appetizers 8

Beverages 9

Small Bites 39

Canapés, Crostini and Sandwiches 83

Stuffed, Wrapped and Rolled 113

Spreads 147

Dips 185

Soups 213

Development Committee 248

Contributors 249

Index 251

Ordering Information 256

"BE WISELY FRUGAL IN THY PREPARATION,

AND FREELY IN THY ENTERTAINMENTS,

IF THY GUESTS BE RIGHT, IT IS ENOUGH, IF NOT,

IT IS TOO MUCH; TOO MUCH IS A VANITY,

ENOUGH IS A FEAST."

Francis Quarles, 17th century

Appetizers started as a Scandinavian custom of serving piquant dishes with "cocktails." Then Russia took the custom and changed it to serving tidbits which would soak up vodka. They are traditionally oily, creamy, or starchy items to abate the effect of alcohol. Ideally, hors d'oeuvres (translated as "that part from the main work") should complement the meal. It would, in fact, be a favor to your dinner guests to only offer them as an aperitif like sherry and feed them thoughtful hors d'oeuvres which would complement—not spoil—their dinner. But for a cocktail party, one must be so didactic; a clever arrangement of meat, fish, sweets, and savories should be displayed. Not all of it should be "finger food." Quiche served with plates satisfies some people better than nineteen small bits, and so therefore even the most parsimonious host can freely serve it.

Bon Appetit!!!!!!

BEVERAGES

*Certain top stables are in the same barn every year, such as
Rodney Jenkins's Hilltop Stables of Orange, Virginia, along with Cismont
Manor of Keswick, Virginia. George Morris's Hunterdon in barn 7A
is also part of the history of the barns at Devon.*

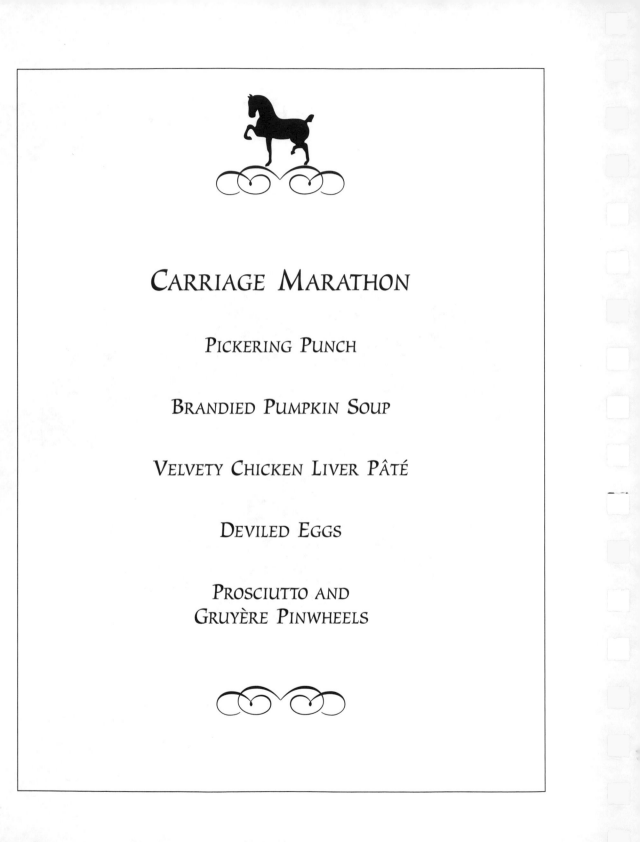

Carriage Marathon

Pickering Punch

Brandied Pumpkin Soup

Velvety Chicken Liver Pâté

Deviled Eggs

Prosciutto and
Gruyère Pinwheels

CHAMPAGNE CUP

Juice of 4 oranges
Juice of 3 lemons
Sugar to taste
2 (750-milliliter) bottles Champagne
¹/₂ cup crème de cassis
¹/₂ cup vermouth
¹/₂ cup golden rum
Cucumber peel
1 large block of ice, or large pieces of ice

Mix the orange juice and lemon juice in a punch bowl and sweeten with sugar. Stir in the Champagne, liqueur, vermouth, rum and cucumber peel. Add the block of ice and let stand for 10 minutes. Ladle into punch cups. **SERVES 10 to 12**

USE LARGE PIECES OF ICE RATHER THAN CUBES SO THEY DO NOT DILUTE TOO QUICKLY.

DEVON DERBY PUNCH

Orange juice
Fresh strawberries
2 (750-milliliter) bottles Champagne
4 quarts ginger ale
¹/₂ gallon orange sherbet
1 (12-ounce) can frozen lemonade concentrate
1 (10-ounce) package frozen strawberries

Fill a ring mold with orange juice and add fresh strawberries. Freeze until solid. Combine the Champagne, ginger ale, sherbet, lemonade concentrate and frozen strawberries in a large silver punch bowl and mix gently. Float the ice ring in the punch. Ladle into punch cups. SERVES **30 to 40**

THIS PUNCH IS SERVED AT THE DEVON DERBY TEA EVERY YEAR!

FISH HOUSE PUNCH

6 cups water
2/3 pound sugar
2 (750-milliliter) bottles dark rum
1 (750-milliliter) bottle Cognac
Juice of 12 lemons
Juice of 12 limes
3/4 cup (6 ounces) peach brandy
1 large block of ice

Make a simple syrup by bringing the water and sugar to a boil in a saucepan and boil until the sugar dissolves. Remove from the heat and let stand until cool.

Combine the simple syrup, rum, Cognac, lemon juice, lime juice and peach brandy in a punch bowl and mix well. Add the block of ice and let stand for 1 hour or longer. Ladle into punch cups and garnish with sprigs of fresh mint. **SERVES 50**

MINT ZINGER PUNCH

2 cups assorted mint leaves
  (peppermint, spearmint, chocolate mint,
    orange mint, apple mint, etc.)
4 cups boiling water
1/4 cup sugar
2 quarts ginger ale
Juice of 2 oranges
Juice of 2 lemons
Sprigs of mint and/or edible flowers

Steep the mint leaves in the boiling water in a heatproof bowl for
15 minutes. Strain into a large container, discarding the solids. Let stand
until cool. Stir in the sugar, ginger ale, orange juice and lemon juice.
  Pour the punch into a punch bowl and add ice. Float sprigs of mint
and/or edible flowers in the punch. Ladle into punch cups. SERVES **10 to 12**

PICKERING PUNCH

6 ounces brandy
3 ounces vodka
1 ounce Kahlúa

Mix the brandy, vodka and liqueur in a small pitcher and pour into a flask,
if desired. Great for fox hunts. SERVES **1 or 2**

Trinidad Rum Punch

SIMPLE SYRUP
2 cups sugar
1 cup water

PUNCH
2 cups rum (1 cup light and 1 cup dark, if desired)
1¹/4 cups strained lime juice
²/3 cup orange juice
4 or 5 drops of angostura bitters
1 dash of grated nutmeg
2 slices pineapple, cut into wedges
2 slices orange, cut into wedges
8 cherries

To prepare the syrup, combine the sugar and water in a saucepan and bring to a boil. Boil for 10 minutes. Remove from the heat and let stand until cool.

To prepare the punch, combine the rum, lime juice, orange juice, 2 tablespoons of the simple syrup and the angostura bitters in a pitcher and mix well. Store the remaining simple syrup in the refrigerator for future use. Fill glasses halfway with cracked ice and pour the punch over the ice. Sprinkle with nutmeg and float one pineapple wedge, one orange wedge and one cherry in each glass. **SERVES 8**

PEACH WHITE WINE SANGRIA

1 cup loosely packed fresh basil leaves
3/4 cup sugar
1/4 cup fresh lemon juice
2 (12-ounce) cans peach nectar
1 (750-milliliter) bottle dry white wine, chilled
1 large peach, peeled and chopped
8 to 10 sprigs of basil

Combine the basil leaves, sugar and lemon juice in a small saucepan and bruise the basil leaves by mashing with a wooden spoon. Add one can of the nectar and bring to a simmer. Simmer until the sugar dissolves, stirring constantly. Remove from the heat and let stand for 5 minutes.

Pour through a medium mesh sieve into a heatproof pitcher, discarding the solids. Stir in the wine, peach, remaining can of peach nectar and the sprigs of basil. Chill, covered, for 1 to 24 hours. Serve over ice in glasses. **SERVES 4 to 6**

Sunny Sangria

3 tablespoons sugar
3 tablespoons spiced dark rum
3 tablespoons Cointreau or
*   other orange-flavored liqueur*
1 orange, sliced
1 lemon, sliced
1 ripe peach, cut into wedges
2 ripe plums, cut into wedges
2 cinnamon sticks
1 (750-milliliter) bottle dry red wine
Club soda (optional)

Combine the sugar, rum and liqueur in a large pitcher and stir until the sugar dissolves. Add the orange, lemon, peach, plums and cinnamon sticks and mix well. Pour in the wine.

Chill, covered, for several hours to allow the flavors to combine. To serve, discard the cinnamon sticks and spoon the sliced fruit into glasses. Pour the sangria over the fruit and top each serving with a splash of club soda. Serve immediately. SERVES 8

PREPARE 1 DAY IN ADVANCE OF SERVING FOR THE BEST FLAVOR. STORE IN THE REFRIGERATOR.

LEE BAILEY'S CHAMPAGNE AND APPLEJACK

1 cup sugar
1/2 cup water
1 ounce applejack
Champagne
1 lemon twist

Make a simple syrup by bringing the sugar and water to a boil in a saucepan and boil until the sugar dissolves. Let stand until cool. Combine 1/2 teaspoon of the simple syrup with the brandy in a flute. Store the remaining simple syrup in the refrigerator for future use. Add enough Champagne to fill the flute and stir gently. Moisten the rim of the flute with the lemon twist and twist over the drink. Float the lemon twist on top. **SERVES 1**

RASPBERRY AND CHAMPAGNE APERITIF

1 1/4 cups frozen unsweetened whole raspberries
3/4 cup Champagne, chilled
2 tablespoons Grand Marnier or
    other orange-flavored liqueur
2 teaspoons crème de cassis

Combine the raspberries, Champagne and liqueurs in a blender and process until smooth. Pour into a tall flute and serve immediately. If desired, strain the drink through a small tea strainer to remove the seeds before serving. **SERVES 1**

BLOODY MARY

1 (32-ounce) bottle clamato juice
3/4 cup (12 ounces) vodka (Absolut Peppar preferred)
1/2 cup lemon juice
1/4 cup Worcestershire sauce
2 tablespoons horseradish
1 1/2 teaspoons sugar
8 dashes of Tabasco sauce from 12-ounce bottle, or
   15 dashes from smaller-size bottle
1 teaspoon (scant) celery salt
1 teaspoon (scant) celery seeds
1/2 teaspoon Jane's Krazy Mixed-Up salt
1/2 teaspoon Old Bay seasoning
1/2 teaspoon freshly ground pepper

Combine the clamato juice, vodka, lemon juice, Worcestershire sauce and horseradish in a large pitcher and mix well. Stir in the sugar, Tabasco sauce, celery salt, celery seeds, Jane's Krazy salt, Old Bay seasoning and pepper. Pour over ice in glasses and garnish each serving with a celery stick. **SERVES 10 to 12**

PLAZA BELLINI

1 handful fresh mint leaves
1 cup sugar
1 (32-ounce) bottle peach juice or apricot juice, chilled
1 (750-milliliter) bottle Champagne, chilled

Reserve four to six mint leaves for garnish. Combine the remaining mint leaves and sugar in a food processor and pulse until of a paste consistency. Dip the rims of four to six Champagne glasses in the mint mixture and rotate gently to cover the rims evenly. Let stand until dry.

Fill the glasses halfway with the peach juice and top off with the Champagne. Garnish each serving with one of the reserved mint leaves. **SERVES 4 to 6**

"I HAVE VOLUNTEERED AT DEVON FOR 73 YEARS, AND I CERTAINLY WASN'T GOING TO LET A CAST ON MY ELBOW KEEP ME FROM DOING MY SHIFT."

—VIOLA BEMENT

WATERMELON DAIQUIRI

4 cups chopped seeded watermelon
1/2 cup light rum
1/4 cup fresh lime juice
1/4 cup orange-flavored liqueur

Arrange the watermelon in a shallow pan and freeze, covered, for 6 hours or longer. Combine the frozen watermelon, rum, lime juice and liqueur in a blender and process until smooth, scraping the side once. Add enough ice cubes to bring the mixture to the 5-cup level and process until smooth. Pour into daiquiri glasses and serve immediately. SERVES 6

DARK 'N STORMY

8 ounces ginger beer
2 ounces rum (Gosling's Black Seal preferred)

Mix the beer and rum in a small pitcher. Pour over ice in a glass. SERVES 1

FRENCH 75

1 sugar cube
3/4 cup Champagne, chilled
2 tablespoons Cognac
Dash of angostura bitters

Place the sugar cube in the bottom of a flute and add the Champagne and brandy. Sprinkle with bitters and serve immediately. SERVES 1

THIS DRINK WAS NAMED AFTER A POWERFUL, SEVENTY-FIVE-MILLIMETER CANNON USED DURING WORLD WAR I.

Palm Beach Flirtini

1 pineapple, cut into chunks
Vodka
1 1/2 ounces vodka
1/2 ounce Cointreau
3 ounces Champagne

Combine the pineapple with enough vodka to cover in a bowl. Marinate, covered, in the refrigerator for 2 weeks, stirring occasionally.

Pour 1 1/2 ounces vodka into a chilled martini glass. Skewer two chunks of the marinated pineapple on a wooden pick and place in the glass. Add the liqueur and top off with the Champagne. Serve immediately.
SERVES 1

Ginger Gale

8 ounces ginger ale
2 ounces rum (Gosling's Black Seal preferred)

Mix the ginger ale and rum in a small pitcher and pour over ice in a glass. Serve immediately. SERVES 1

PINEAPPLE GREYHOUND

1 ounce vodka
2 ounces fresh pineapple juice
1 1/2 ounces fresh pink grapefruit juice

Fill a rocks glass or large tumbler with ice cubes to the rim. Add the vodka, pineapple juice and grapefruit juice and stir until combined. Garnish with two half-moon slices of grapefruit. SERVES 1

THE CLASSIC COCKTAIL KNOWN AS A GREYHOUND COMBINES VODKA AND GRAPEFRUIT JUICE. STIR IN FRESH PINEAPPLE JUICE AS WELL. PREPARING YOUR OWN FRESH JUICES ENSURES AN EXCEPTIONALLY DELICIOUS DRINK.

KAHLÚA

4 cups water
3 cups sugar
2 tablespoons instant coffee granules
2¹/₂ cups 100-proof vodka
1 teaspoon vanilla extract

Bring the water, sugar and coffee granules to a boil in a saucepan and reduce the heat. Simmer for 2¹/₂ hours. Remove from the heat and let stand until cool. Stir in the vodka and vanilla. Pour into a bottle and seal. Let stand for 1 week or longer before serving. **SERVES 6**

STORE UNDER YOUR FAVORITE SOFA SO YOU CAN SPIN THE BOTTLE EACH TIME YOU SIT THERE.

DEVON JULEP

1 (28-ounce) bottle bourbon
6 ounces white crème de menthe
4 ounces vodka

Combine the bourbon, liqueur and vodka in a pitcher and mix well. Pour over ice in glasses. Garnish each serving with a sprig of mint. SERVES 4 to 5

CRANBERRY KIR ROYALE

1/2 cup thawed frozen cranberry juice
cocktail concentrate
1 1/3 cups Champagne, chilled

Pour 2 tablespoons of the cranberry juice concentrate into each of four chilled Champagne glasses. Add 1/3 cup of Champagne to each glass and serve immediately. SERVES 4

LATINOPOLITAN

6 ounces Bacardi Limón rum
2 ounces Triple Sec
1/4 cup lime juice
2 1/2 tablespoons cranberry juice
4 mint leaves

Place several ice cubes in a cocktail shaker and add the rum, liqueur, lime juice and cranberry juice. Shake until chilled. Strain into four chilled martini glasses and float a mint leaf on top of each. **SERVES 4**

MARVELOUS MARGARITA I

4 teaspoons grated lime zest
1/2 cup fresh lime juice (4 or 5 limes)
4 teaspoons grated lemon zest
1/2 cup fresh lemon juice (4 or 5 lemons)
1/4 cup superfine sugar
Pinch of salt
2 cups crushed ice
1 cup tequila (Reposado preferred)
1 cup Triple Sec

Mix the lime zest, lime juice, lemon zest, lemon juice, sugar and salt in a large glass measuring cup. Chill, covered with plastic wrap, for 4 to 24 hours.

Divide 1 cup of the crushed ice evenly between four to six margarita glasses or double old-fashioned glasses. Strain the zest mixture into a 1-quart pitcher or cocktail shaker. Add the tequila, liqueur and remaining crushed ice. Stir or shake until combined and chilled. Strain into the ice-filled glasses. Serve immediately. **SERVES 4 to 6**

Marvelous Margarita II

3 cups fresh lime juice
1¼ cups superfine sugar
3 cups tequila (Agave preferred)
⅓ cup Triple Sec

Combine the lime juice and sugar in a pitcher and let stand until the sugar dissolves, stirring occasionally. Add the tequila, liqueur and ice and stir until chilled. Strain into salt-rimmed margarita glasses. **Serves 6**

Watermelon Margarita

Salt to taste (optional)
2 lime wedges (optional)
2 cups chopped seeded watermelon
4 ounces tequila
¼ cup fresh lime juice
1 ounce Cointreau or other orange-flavored liqueur

Spread salt on a small flat plate. Moisten the rims of two margarita glasses with the lime wedges. Invert the glasses onto the plate and rotate gently to cover the rims evenly with the salt, shaking off the excess.

Combine the watermelon, tequila, lime juice, liqueur and ice cubes in a blender and process until puréed. Pour into the salt-rimmed glasses and garnish each serving with a lime slice. **Serves 2**

CHOCOLATE MARTINI

2 1/2 cups vodka, chilled
1 1/4 cups chocolate liqueur
1/4 cup raspberry liqueur
1/3 cup half-and-half (optional)
Chocolate syrup
Sweetened baking cocoa (Ghirardelli preferred)

Combine the vodka, liqueurs and half-and-half in a pitcher and stir until well mixed. Chill for 1 hour or longer.

Fill eight to ten martini glasses with ice and let stand for 5 minutes. Discard the ice. Dip the rims of the chilled martini glasses in chocolate syrup and then dip in baking cocoa to coat. Pour the vodka mixture into the glasses and serve immediately. SERVES **8 to 10**

THIS MAKES A GREAT AFTER-DINNER DRINK.

DEVON BLUE RIBBON MARTINI

2 ounces premium vodka
2 ounces blue raspberry juice (Rose's preferred)

Combine the vodka, raspberry juice and ice in a martini pitcher and stir until chilled. Serve on the rocks or straight up and garnish with fresh or frozen raspberries. SERVES 1

EVEN IF YOU HAVE NEVER WON A DEVON BLUE, AFTER A FEW OF THESE YOU WON'T CARE!!!

Espresso Martini

2 ounces fresh brewed espresso
1 ounce good-quality vodka
3/4 ounce Kahlúa
3/4 ounce Tia Maria

Fill a cocktail shaker with ice and add the espresso, vodka and liqueurs. Shake until combined and chilled. Strain into a martini glass and serve immediately. SERVES 1

THIS RECIPE HAS NEVER BEEN PUBLISHED AND UP UNTIL NOW WAS A WELL-GUARDED SECRET OF TOM HINDLEY, THE ASSISTANT MANAGER AT PRIMAVERA RISTORANTE.

WATERMELON MARTINI

1¹/2 ounces vodka
¹/2 ounce lime juice
¹/2 ounce Cointreau
¹/2 ounce Chambord
6 (¹/2-inch) cubes frozen watermelon

Fill a cocktail shaker half full of ice. Add the vodka, lime juice, liqueurs and watermelon and shake for 30 seconds or until chilled. Strain into a chilled martini glass. SERVES 1

POMEGRANATE MOJITO

1 cup sugar
¹/2 cup water
12 fresh spearmint leaves
Juice of ¹/2 lime
1¹/2 ounces white rum
7 ounces club soda
¹/2 to 1 ounce pomegranate juice

Make a simple syrup by bringing the sugar and water to a boil in a saucepan and boil until the sugar dissolves. Let stand until cool.

Gently crush the mint leaves in a tall chilled glass and add the lime juice. Pour 2 tablespoons of the simple syrup over the mint leaves and fill the glass with crushed ice. Add the rum, club soda and pomegranate juice and stir until combined. Garnish with a lime wedge and a few sprigs of spearmint. Store the remaining simple syrup in the refrigerator for future use. SERVES 1

STONE FENCE

2 to 3 ounces hard cider
1 1/2 ounces bourbon or rye whiskey
1/4 ounce crème de cassis
Dash of angostura bitters

Combine the cider, bourbon, liqueur and bitters in a cocktail shaker and shake to mix. Pour over ice cubes in a highball glass or double old-fashioned glass. Garnish with a lemon twist. SERVES 1

UNION LEAGUE COCKTAIL

1 ounce rye whiskey
1/2 ounce Jamaican rum (Myers's preferred)
1 ounce lemon juice
1 ounce orange juice
1/2 ounce Triple Sec
1 tablespoon sugar

Combine the whiskey, rum, lemon juice, orange juice, liqueur and sugar in a cocktail shaker and shake until the sugar dissolves. Pour over ice in a glass. SERVES 1

BUBBLE COFFEE

¹/₂ ounce Tia Maria
¹/₂ ounce amaretto
¹/₂ ounce Kahlúa
1 mug of hot black coffee (regular or decaffeinated)
Grand Marnier
Whipped cream

Add the Tia Maria, amaretto and Kahlúa to the coffee and stir until combined. Carefully float the Grand Marnier over the coffee and top with a dollop of whipped cream. Serve immediately. **SERVES 1**

IRISH COFFEE

1 jigger Irish whiskey (do not substitute)
3 sugar cubes
Hot strong black coffee
Whipped cream

Heat a stemmed whiskey goblet. Pour in the whiskey and add the sugar cubes. Add coffee to within 1 inch of the rim and stir until the sugar dissolves. Top with whipped cream slightly aerated so that the cream floats on top. Do not stir after adding the whipped cream as the true flavor is obtained by drinking the hot Irish coffee through the cream. **SERVES 1**

WASSAIL

8 crab apples
1 cup good ale
Brown sugar
7 cups good ale
¹/₂ bottle sherry
¹/₂ teaspoon ginger
¹/₂ teaspoon nutmeg
¹/₂ teaspoon cinnamon
2 strips of lemon zest
Toast (optional)

Arrange the crab apples in a baking pan. Add enough water to measure 1 inch. Drizzle with 1 cup ale and sprinkle with brown sugar. Bake at 350 degrees for about 45 minutes or until tender.

Combine 7 cups ale, the sherry, ginger, nutmeg, cinnamon and lemon zest in a saucepan and simmer for 5 minutes. Pour into a heatproof punch bowl and top with the crab apples and toast. Serve hot in mugs.
SERVES 6 to 12

"BE WELL" IS WHAT WASSAIL ORIGINALLY MEANT WHEN ANGLO-SAXONS DRANK TO EACH OTHER'S HEALTH. WASSAIL WAS SERVED DURING THE 12 DAYS OF CHRISTMAS. A GREAT TREAT OF THE WASSAIL BOWL WAS THE TOAST THAT SWAM IN THE ALE. CONSUMED WITH EXPRESSIONS OF GOOD WISHES, IT GAVE RISE TO THE CUSTOM OF "DRINKING A TOAST."

Iced Tea Four Ways

8 cups boiling water
8 tea bags

Pour the water into a heatproof pitcher and add the tea bags. Let steep for 10 minutes. Discard the tea bags and let cool to room temperature before storing in the refrigerator.

For variety, add one of the following flavor boosters and pour over ice in glasses.

GINGER AND HONEY:

Add 2 teaspoons freshly grated ginger and $1/3$ cup honey. Strain, if desired.

POMEGRANATE JUICE AND LIME:

Add 2 cups pomegranate juice, 3 thinly sliced limes and $1/4$ cup sugar.

WATERMELON AND BASIL:

Add $1/8$ medium watermelon, seeded and cut into small triangles, and 1 small bunch basil sprigs. Sweeten with sugar, if desired.

PEACH AND MINT:

Add 4 ripe peaches cut into $1/2$-inch pieces and 1 small bunch mint sprigs. Sweeten with sugar, if desired. **SERVES 8**

Blueberry Mint Lemonade

MINT SYRUP
2³/4 cups water
1 cup sugar
2 bunches mint, trimmed and cut into
*   2-inch lengths*

LEMONADE
1 pint blueberries
³/4 cup plus 2 tablespoons fresh lemon juice
*   (about 5 lemons)*

To prepare the syrup, bring the water, sugar and mint to a boil in a small tall saucepan over medium-high heat. Boil until the sugar dissolves, stirring constantly. Remove from the heat and let stand for 30 minutes. Pour through a fine sieve into a bowl, discarding the solids. Store in an airtight container for up to 2 months.

To prepare the lemonade, process the blueberries and lemon juice in a food processor until puréed. Press the purée through a fine sieve into a pitcher, discarding the pulp. Stir in 1¹/2 cups of the syrup. Pour over ice in glasses. Garnish each serving with additional blueberries and sprigs of mint. **SERVES 6**

MOCK MARGARITAS

1 (12-ounce) can frozen lemonade concentrate, thawed
1 (12-ounce) can frozen limeade concentrate, thawed
1 cup confectioners' sugar
6 cups crushed ice
Lime wedges
Coarse salt
1 (1-liter) bottle club soda, chilled

Process the lemonade concentrate, limeade concentrate, confectioners' sugar and crushed ice half at a time in a blender until smooth. Pour both batches into a 4-quart plastic container and freeze until firm.

Rub the rims of stemmed glasses with lime wedges. Place salt in a saucer and gently rotate the rim of each glass in the salt until coated. Remove the margarita mixture from the freezer 30 minutes before serving. Add the club soda and stir until slushy. Pour into the salt-rimmed glasses. **MAKES 3 quarts**

SMALL BITES

*The Devon Horse Show took place on
the grounds of The Devon Inn in 1898.*

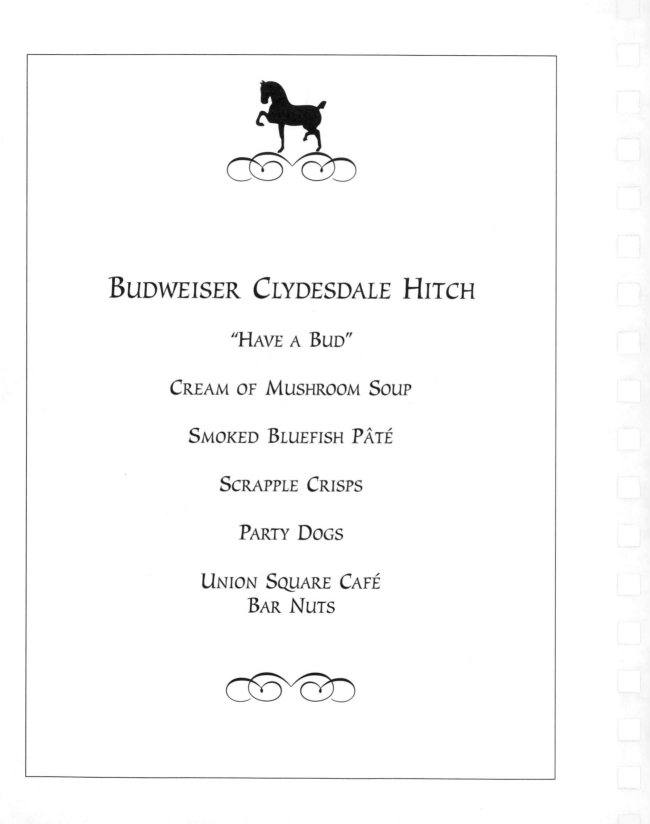

BUDWEISER CLYDESDALE HITCH

"HAVE A BUD"

CREAM OF MUSHROOM SOUP

SMOKED BLUEFISH PÂTÉ

SCRAPPLE CRISPS

PARTY DOGS

UNION SQUARE CAFÉ
BAR NUTS

CRAB CLAWS WITH MUSTARD SAUCE

1/2 cup mayonnaise
1 1/2 teaspoons Dijon mustard
1/2 teaspoon dry mustard
1/2 teaspoon Worcestershire sauce
1 (8- or 10-ounce) can crab claws, drained

Combine the mayonnaise, Dijon mustard, dry mustard and Worcestershire sauce in a bowl and mix well. Store, covered, in the refrigerator for 1 hour or longer to allow the flavors to blend. Serve with the crab claws. SERVES **6 to 8**

DO NOT FORGET TO PUT OUT AN EXTRA BOWL FOR THE CLAW SHELLS.

BLUE MUSSELS, PERNOD AND THYME

1 pound mussels
1 tablespoon olive oil
1 cup mirepoix (1/2 cup finely chopped onion,
   1/4 cup finely chopped carrot and
   1/4 cup finely chopped celery)
1 tablespoon chopped garlic
1/4 cup fresh thyme leaves
Salt and freshly ground white pepper to taste
3 ounces Pernod
1/2 cup water
1/2 cup (1 stick) unsalted butter

Scrub the mussels and discard any mussels without tightly closed shells. Heat a stainless steel sauté pan over medium heat and add the olive oil, mirepoix, garlic and thyme. Sauté for 1 minute. Add the mussels and season heavily with salt and white pepper. Remove from the heat and add the liqueur. Carefully ignite with a long match and allow the flames to subside.

Return the pan to the stove over high heat. Add the water and butter and steam for 3 minutes or until the shells open, stirring frequently. Arrange the mussels in four to six warm serving bowls. Ladle the cooking broth and vegetables evenly over the mussels. Garnish each serving with chopped Italian parsley and crostini. **SERVES 4 to 6**

THIS RECIPE IS COURTESY OF ANDREW DEERY, CHEF/OWNER OF MAJOLICA RESTAURANT IN PHOENIXVILLE, PA.

Bloody Mary Oysters

1¹/₂ cups vegetable juice cocktail
3 tablespoons vodka
1¹/₂ tablespoons fresh lime juice
4 to 6 drops of Tabasco sauce
1 teaspoon Worcestershire sauce
Celery salt to taste
White pepper to taste
1 cucumber, finely chopped
2 ribs celery, finely chopped
12 oysters on the half shell
1 lemon, cut into wedges

Combine the vegetable juice cocktail, vodka, lime juice, Tabasco sauce, Worcestershire sauce, celery salt and white pepper in a blender and process until blended. Mix the cucumber and celery in a small bowl.

Fill a shallow rectangular dish with crushed ice and arrange the oysters on the ice. Spoon the vodka mixture evenly over the oysters and sprinkle with the cucumber mixture. Arrange the lemon wedges around the oyster shells.
Makes 1 dozen

These oysters are dressed to impress.

OYSTER CROQUETTES

1 pint oysters, drained
1/2 cup soft bread crumbs
1/2 cup (2 ounces) freshly grated Parmesan cheese
1 tablespoon minced parsley
1 teaspoon Dijon mustard
1 teaspoon grated onion
1/2 teaspoon Tabasco sauce
1/4 teaspoon salt
1/4 teaspoon pepper
1 egg, beaten
2 teaspoons butter, melted
1 egg, beaten
1 cup dry bread crumbs
Peanut oil for deep-frying

Pour boiling water over the oysters in a colander and drain. Finely chop the oysters. Combine the oysters, soft bread crumbs, cheese, parsley, Dijon mustard, onion, Tabasco sauce, salt and pepper in a bowl and mix well. Stir in one egg and the butter. Chill, covered, for 20 to 30 minutes.

Shape the oyster mixture into 1-inch balls. Dip the balls in one egg and coat with the dry bread crumbs. Heat the peanut oil to 360 degrees in a deep skillet. Add the croquettes to the hot oil and fry until brown on all sides. Drain on paper towels. Serve warm with your favorite dipping sauce. **SERVES 4 to 6**

Scallop Cakes with Cilantro Mayonnaise

CILANTRO MAYONNAISE
3/4 cup mayonnaise
1/2 cup finely chopped
cilantro leaves
2 tablespoons lime juice
1 teaspoon Dijon mustard
1/2 teaspoon minced garlic
2 dashes of sherry pepper sauce
(Outerbridge preferred)

SCALLOP CAKES
1 tablespoon olive oil
1/2 cup finely chopped onion

1 pound sea scallops,
coarsely chopped
1/4 cup chopped fresh chives
1 tablespoon chopped fresh parsley
1 tablespoon all-purpose flour
1 tablespoon minced fresh ginger
1 tablespoon lime juice
1 egg, beaten
1 teaspoon finely grated lime zest
2 tablespoons panko
Panko for breading
Canola oil

To prepare the cilantro mayonnaise, combine the mayonnaise, cilantro, lime juice, Dijon mustard, garlic and pepper sauce in a bowl and mix well. Chill, covered, until serving time. Bring to room temperature before serving.

To prepare the cakes, heat the olive oil in a sauté pan and add the onion. Cook for 4 to 5 minutes or until tender. Let stand until cool. Combine the onion and scallops in a large bowl. Stir in the chives, parsley, flour, ginger, lime juice, egg, lime zest and 2 tablespoons panko, mixing well after each addition. Chill, covered, for 1 hour or longer.

Shape the scallop mixture into 1-inch cakes. Gently roll each cake in a small amount of panko on a sheet of waxed paper. Cook in canola oil in a skillet over medium heat for 3 minutes per side or until brown; drain on paper towels. Serve warm topped with the mayonnaise. **SERVES 4 to 6**

SCALLOPS ROCKEFELLER

12 oyster shells, rinsed and patted dry
2 tablespoons unsalted butter
4 ounces flat-leaf spinach
Salt and freshly ground pepper to taste
1/2 cup crème fraîche or sour cream, drained
2 tablespoons horseradish, drained
12 sea scallops, patted dry
1/4 cup (1 ounce) freshly grated Parmesan cheese
1/4 cup bread crumbs
1 teaspoon freshly ground pepper

Arrange the oyster shells in a single layer on a baking sheet. Heat the butter in a large sauté pan over medium-high heat and add the spinach, salt and pepper to taste. Cook for 2 minutes or just until the spinach wilts. Remove the spinach to a colander and press the spinach with the back of a wooden spoon to remove the excess moisture.

Whisk the crème fraîche and horseradish in a bowl until combined. Season with salt and pepper to taste and fold in the spinach. Spoon a scant tablespoon of the mixture in each oyster shell. Top each with one scallop and season with salt and pepper to taste.

Mix the cheese, bread crumbs and 1 teaspoon pepper in a bowl. Divide the cheese mixture evenly among the scallops. Broil for 2 to 3 minutes or until golden brown. Serve immediately. **MAKES 1 dozen**

SAUCY SCALLOPS

¹/₃ cup lemon juice
3 tablespoons honey
3 tablespoons Dijon mustard
2 tablespoons olive oil
¹/₂ teaspoon curry powder
1 pound bay scallops

Combine the lemon juice, honey, Dijon mustard, olive oil and curry powder in a bowl and mix well. Add the scallops and toss to coat. Let stand for 15 minutes.

Heat the scallop mixture in a large skillet. Cook until the scallops turn opaque and start to brown, stirring constantly. Skewer each scallop with a wooden pick and serve. SERVES **6 to 8**

MEXICAN SEAFOOD COCKTAIL

1¹/₂ cups clamato juice, chilled
¹/₂ cup finely chopped white onion
¹/₄ cup cilantro
¹/₄ cup ketchup
¹/₄ cup fresh lime juice
Hot sauce to taste
1 teaspoon salt
1 avocado, chopped
8 ounces fresh jumbo lump crab meat, drained and flaked
4 ounces cooked shrimp, cut into chunks

Combine the clamato juice, onion, cilantro, ketchup, lime juice, hot sauce and salt in a pitcher and mix well. Divide the avocado, crab meat and shrimp evenly between four glasses. Pour the clamato juice mixture over the top of each serving. Serve immediately. SERVES **4**

Buffalo Shrimp

BUFFALO SAUCE

6 ounces Louisiana hot sauce
   (Pete's or Crystal preferred)
2¹⁄₂ tablespoons butter
1 teaspoon Tabasco sauce
1 teaspoon cayenne pepper

SHRIMP

2 cups all-purpose flour
2 tablespoons Creole seasoning or
   Old Bay seasoning

1 tablespoon garlic powder
2 teaspoons cayenne pepper
2 teaspoons freshly ground
   black pepper
1 teaspoon onion powder
1 pound large (21- to 25-count)
   shrimp, peeled with tails
   intact and deveined
4 cups vegetable oil for frying

To prepare the sauce, combine the hot sauce, butter, Tabasco sauce and cayenne pepper in a saucepan. Cook over medium-low heat until the butter melts, stirring occasionally. Cover to keep warm.

To prepare the shrimp, combine the flour, Creole seasoning, garlic powder, cayenne pepper, black pepper and onion powder in a sealable plastic bag and seal tightly. Shake to combine the ingredients. Place the shrimp in a colander and rinse with cold water. Add to the flour mixture and seal the bag. Shake until the shrimp are coated, reserving the remaining flour mixture. Arrange the shrimp in a single layer on a baking sheet and chill for 15 to 20 minutes. Coat the shrimp in the flour mixture a second time.

Fry the shrimp in 375-degree oil in a deep fryer for 2 to 3 minutes or until the shrimp turn pink. Immediately drain in a colander or bowl lined with paper towels. Remove to another bowl and add the warm sauce, stirring to coat the shrimp completely. Serve with blue cheese dressing and celery sticks.

Another option is to sauté the shrimp. Pour enough oil into a large skillet to coat the bottom and heat over medium-high heat. Arrange the shrimp in a single layer; do not crowd. Sauté for 2 minutes on the first side. Turn with tongs and sauté for 1 minute longer or until the shrimp turn pink. **SERVES 4 to 6**

SEVICHE WITH SHRIMP AND AVOCADO

1¹/2 pounds deveined peeled large shrimp
Juice of 5 limes
2 tablespoons minced red onion
1 tablespoon minced seeded jalapeño chile
Salt to taste
2 avocados, chopped
1 cucumber, peeled, seeded and chopped
1 bunch cilantro, trimmed and chopped
2 tablespoons minced red onion
1 tablespoon minced seeded jalapeño chile

Place the shrimp in a colander and rinse with cold water; pat dry. Toss the shrimp, lime juice, 2 tablespoons onion, 1 tablespoon jalapeño chile and salt in a bowl until coated. Pour into a sealable plastic bag. Press out the air and seal tightly. Chill for 1 hour or until the shrimp are opaque, turning occasionally to distribute the lime juice.

Toss with the avocados, cucumber, cilantro, 2 tablespoons onion and 1 tablespoon jalapeño chile in a bowl. Taste and adjust the salt. Serve with tortilla chips. **SERVES 12 to 15**

"DEVON IS . . . THE JOY OF BEING SURROUNDED BY WONDERFUL PEOPLE WHO ARE WORKING FOR A BEAUTIFUL CAUSE."

—MOLLY SOMERS

SHRIMP AND ARTICHOKES

1 cup vegetable oil
1 cup apple cider vinegar
1/4 cup sugar
1/4 cup water
2 tablespoons Worcestershire sauce
1 1/2 tablespoons lemon juice
1 tablespoon salt
1/4 teaspoon dry mustard
1/4 teaspoon garlic powder
3 bay leaves
2 (14-ounce) cans water-pack artichoke hearts
1 (5-ounce) can pitted black olives
1 Spanish onion, thinly sliced
1 lemon, thinly sliced
3 pounds large shrimp, peeled, deveined and cooked

Whisk the oil, vinegar, sugar, water, Worcestershire sauce, lemon juice, salt, dry mustard, garlic powder and bay leaves in a large bowl until combined. Stir in the artichokes, olives, onion and lemon. Add the shrimp and toss to coat.

Marinate, covered, in the refrigerator for 8 to 10 hours, stirring every 2 hours. Discard the bay leaves and drain some of the liquid just before serving. Serve in a glass bowl with wooden picks. **SERVES 25**

Cinco de Mayo Shrimp Cocktail

4 plum tomatoes, coarsely chopped
1/2 red onion, sliced
1/4 cup fresh lime juice
1/4 cup chopped fresh cilantro
1 jalapeño chile, seeded
2 garlic cloves
2 teaspoons sugar
1/2 teaspoon salt
1/4 teaspoon chili powder
1/4 teaspoon pepper
6 cups water
30 large fresh shrimp
1 large avocado, chopped

Process the tomatoes, onion, lime juice, cilantro, jalapeño chile, garlic, sugar, salt, chili powder and pepper in a blender or food processor until smooth, scraping the side occasionally. Chill, covered, for up to 1 week.

Bring the water to a boil in a large saucepan and add the shrimp. Boil for 2 to 3 minutes or just until the shrimp turn pink. Drain and rinse with cold water. Chill, covered, for up to 24 hours. Peel and devein the shrimp, leaving the tails intact.

Stir the avocado into the cocktail sauce. Spoon the sauce evenly into six chilled martini glasses or small bowls. Arrange five shrimp around the edge of each glass. Garnish with lime slices. Serve with lime-flavored tortilla chips.
Serves 6

GRILLED SHRIMP SPANISH STYLE

1 cup dry white wine
1 cup olive oil
¹/₂ cup chopped fresh basil
¹/₄ cup fresh lemon juice
2 tablespoons Dijon mustard
Freshly cracked black pepper to taste
24 jumbo shrimp, peeled with tails intact and deveined
24 large whole basil leaves
24 thin slices serrano ham, fat trimmed

Combine the wine, olive oil, chopped basil, lemon juice, Dijon mustard and pepper in a bowl and mix well. Pour over the shrimp in a shallow dish, turning to coat. Marinate, covered, in the refrigerator for 3 hours or longer, turning the shrimp occasionally.

Preheat the grill with a generous amount of mesquite. Drain the shrimp, reserving the marinade. Wrap the middle of each shrimp with one whole basil leaf and then with one slice of the ham. Thread four shrimp lengthwise starting at the head on each of six metal skewers. Grill for several minutes on each side or until the shrimp turn pink, basting with the reserved marinade. Serve immediately. **SERVES 6 for main course or 8 for appetizers**

SPICY GRILLED SHRIMP

1/2 cup olive oil
1/2 cup finely chopped basil
4 garlic cloves, crushed
2 tablespoons white wine vinegar
1 tablespoon Worcestershire sauce
1 1/2 teaspoons Tabasco sauce
1/2 teaspoon salt
1/2 teaspoon pepper
2 pounds large shrimp, peeled and deveined

Whisk the olive oil, basil, garlic, vinegar, Worcestershire sauce, Tabasco sauce, salt and pepper in a bowl. Add the shrimp and toss to coat. Or, combine with the shrimp in a sealable plastic bag.

Marinate, covered, in the refrigerator for 30 minutes to 2 1/2 hours, stirring occasionally; drain. Thread the shrimp on metal skewers and grill over hot coals for 2 1/2 minutes per side or until the shrimp turn pink; do not over cook. Slide the shrimp off the skewers and serve with wooden picks. **SERVES 8**

THIS RECIPE CAN BE EASILY DOUBLED. IT IS GREAT SERVED CHILLED.

Marinated Shrimp with Dipping Sauce

SHRIMP
1/2 cup vinegar
1/4 cup vegetable oil
1 small onion, minced
2 tablespoons chopped parsley
1 garlic clove, minced
Dash of Tabasco sauce
Dash of dill weed
1 pound cooked shrimp

DIPPING SAUCE
1/2 cup mayonnaise
1/4 cup sour cream
1/4 cup ketchup
1/2 teaspoon soy sauce
1/4 teaspoon thyme
1/8 teaspoon paprika
Pinch of garlic powder

To prepare the shrimp, whisk the vinegar, oil, onion, parsley, garlic, Tabasco sauce and dill weed in a bowl until combined. Pour into a sealable plastic bag and add the shrimp. Seal tightly, turning to coat. Marinate in the refrigerator for 8 to 10 hours, turning occasionally; drain.

To prepare the sauce, combine the mayonnaise, sour cream, ketchup, soy sauce, thyme, paprika and garlic powder in a bowl and mix well. Serve with the shrimp. **SERVES 8 to 10**

"FOUR GENERATIONS OF MY FAMILY HAVE ENJOYED THE FRIENDSHIPS MADE AT DEVON."

—NANCY LIGGET

PICKLED SHRIMP

2 1/2 pounds shrimp
1/2 cup coarsely chopped celery tops
1/4 cup pickling spices
3 1/2 teaspoons salt
1 large onion, sliced
8 ounces whole mushrooms, trimmed
4 to 6 bay leaves
1 1/4 cups vegetable oil
3/4 cup vinegar (1/2 white vinegar and 1/2 wine vinegar)
2 1/2 tablespoons undrained capers
2 1/2 teaspoons celery seeds
Dash of Tabasco sauce, or to taste

Bring a stockpot of water to a boil and add the shrimp, celery tops, pickling spices and salt. Boil for 10 to 12 minutes or until the shrimp turn pink. Drain in a colander and rinse with cold water until cool. Peel and devein the shrimp under cold running water.

Layer the shrimp, onion, mushrooms and bay leaves in a shallow dish. Mix the oil, vinegar, capers, celery seeds and Tabasco sauce in a bowl and pour over the layers. Marinate, covered, in the refrigerator for 24 hours or longer. Discard the bay leaves before serving. You may store in the refrigerator for up to 1 week. **MAKES a variable amount**

POACHED SALMON WITH DILL SAUCE

DILL SAUCE
1/2 cup mayonnaise
2 tablespoons Dijon mustard
2 tablespoons chopped fresh dill weed
1 tablespoon capers

SALMON
1/2 cup soy sauce
1/2 cup white wine
1/2 cup fresh dill weed, chopped
2 tablespoons capers
2 tablespoons sesame oil
8 ounces salmon

To prepare the sauce, combine the mayonnaise, Dijon mustard, dill weed and capers in a bowl and mix well. Chill, covered, until serving time.

To prepare the salmon, mix the soy sauce, wine, dill weed, capers and sesame oil in a shallow baking dish. Add the salmon and turn to coat. Marinate, covered, in the refrigerator for 8 to 10 hours, turning occasionally.

Poach the salmon in the marinade at 400 degrees for 20 to 30 minutes or until the salmon flakes easily. Let stand until cool and arrange the salmon on a serving platter. Serve with the sauce and saltine crackers. **SERVES 8 to 10**

Tuna Skewers with Wasabi Mayonnaise

WASABI MAYONNAISE
2 tablespoons wasabi powder
1 1/2 tablespoons water
1/2 cup mayonnaise

TUNA
1 pound fresh tuna steaks, cut into 3/4-inch cubes
2 1/2 tablespoons soy sauce
28 large slices pickled ginger
1 bunch watercress, trimmed
1 teaspoon freshly ground pepper
1 tablespoon vegetable oil

To prepare the mayonnaise, mix the wasabi powder and water in a small bowl until blended. Whisk in the mayonnaise. Chill, covered, for 30 minutes. May be prepared up to 1 day in advance and stored, covered, in the refrigerator.

To prepare the tuna, toss the tuna and soy sauce in a bowl until coated. Marinate at room temperature for 30 minutes, stirring occasionally. Thread each ginger slice on an 8-inch wooden skewer 2 inches from the tip.

Line a serving platter with the watercress. Place the bowl of mayonnaise in the center of the platter. Drain the tuna and pat dry. Return the tuna to the bowl and sprinkle with the pepper, tossing to coat.

Heat the oil in a large skillet over medium-high heat. Sear the tuna in the hot oil for 2 minutes or until brown on all sides but pink inside. Thread one cube of tuna next to the ginger slice on each prepared skewer. Arrange the skewers over the watercress and serve immediately. **SERVES 8 to 10**

BE SURE TO USE FRESH WASABI POWDER FOR THE WASABI MAYONNAISE AS THE WASABI POWDER CAN TURN BITTER OVER TIME. PICKLED GINGER IS AVAILABLE AT JAPANESE MARKETS.

Hawaiian Beef Sticks

1 cup soy sauce
¹/₄ cup sugar
2 tablespoons red wine vinegar
2 small onions, chopped
1 (2-inch) piece fresh ginger, sliced
2 garlic cloves, crushed
¹/₂ cup water
4 teaspoons cornstarch
2 pounds beef sirloin, cut into thin strips

Combine the soy sauce, sugar, vinegar, onions, ginger and garlic in a small saucepan. Cook over medium heat for 20 minutes or until slightly thickened, stirring occasionally. Mix the water and cornstarch in a small bowl until blended. Add to the soy sauce mixture gradually, stirring constantly.

Cook until the sauce is clear and thickened. Strain through a sieve into a large bowl, pressing out all the juices. Discard the solids and let the sauce stand until cool.

Add the beef to the sauce and stir until coated. Marinate, covered, in the refrigerator for 2 hours, stirring occasionally. Thread two or three beef strips on each of forty-eight metal skewers. Grill over hot coals or broil until the desired degree of doneness. **MAKES 4 dozen sticks**

THE SAUCE MAY BE PREPARED UP TO 1 DAY IN ADVANCE.

Beef Jerky

20 ounces Pepsi
15 ounces soy sauce
15 ounces teriyaki sauce
5 ounces liquid smoke
6 tablespoons dark molasses, or to taste
3 tablespoons dark brown sugar, or to taste
3 tablespoons garlic powder, or to taste
1 tablespoon onion powder, or to taste
1 tablespoon cayenne pepper, or to taste
5 pounds lean beef, such as brisket or rump (cheaper cuts)

Mix the Pepsi, soy sauce, teriyaki sauce, liquid smoke, molasses, brown sugar, garlic powder, onion powder and cayenne pepper in a bowl. Trim as much fat as possible from the beef. Slice the beef with a sharp knife or meat slicer into $1/8$-inch slices.

Pour some of the marinade in the bottom of a plastic or glass rectangular dish. Arrange some of the beef slices over the marinade. Pour more of the marinade over the beef and continue the process until all of the beef is covered with the marinade. Marinate, covered, in the refrigerator for 24 to 48 hours, stirring two to four times.

To dry the beef, place a foil-lined baking sheet on the bottom oven rack to catch the drippings. Thread the slices on metal skewers and hang perpendicular between grates of the oven rack; do not allow the skewers to touch. Dry at 160 to 180 degrees for 3 to 6 hours, depending on the thickness of the slices. Leave the oven door slightly ajar during the drying process. The jerky is ready when the beef slices bend and you can break off a piece easily, not until they are crisp and break. Let stand until cool and store in sealable plastic bags.
Makes 5 pounds

COCKTAIL FRANKS IN BOURBON SAUCE

2 tablespoons butter
1 small onion, finely chopped
1/2 cup bourbon
3/4 cup packed dark brown sugar
2 tablespoons cider vinegar
1 cup ketchup
1 tablespoon Worcestershire sauce
1 teaspoon Tabasco sauce
1 (14- to 16-ounce) package cocktail franks

Melt the butter in a saucepan over medium heat. Add the onion and sauté until tender but not brown. Remove from the heat and stir in the bourbon. Return to the heat and cook for 1 minute longer, stirring occasionally. Add the brown sugar and vinegar and cook until blended, stirring constantly. Mix in the ketchup, Worcestershire sauce and Tabasco sauce.

Cook until heated through. Taste and add additional bourbon and brown sugar, if desired. Add the franks and stir until coated. Let stand until the franks warm in the sauce and serve. **SERVES 10**

SCRAPPLE CRISPS

1 pound scrapple

Slice the scrapple into 1/4-inch slices. Cut each slice into quarters. Arrange the quarters in a single layer on a greased baking sheet. Bake at 375 degrees for about 45 minutes or until brown and crisp. **MAKES 80 crisps**

MAY BE SERVED WITH APPLESAUCE FOR A DIP. MEN ESPECIALLY LIKE THESE CRISPS.

CHEESY BACON PUFFS

1 1/2 cups all-purpose flour
1/2 teaspoon salt
1/4 teaspoon pepper
1/8 teaspoon garlic powder
1 1/2 cups water
1/2 cup (1 stick) butter or margarine
6 eggs
2 cups (8 ounces) shredded sharp Cheddar cheese
8 slices bacon, crisp-cooked and crumbled

Mix the flour, salt, pepper and garlic powder together. Bring the water and butter to a boil in a heavy saucepan. Add the flour mixture and cook for 5 minutes or until the mixture leaves the side of the pan and forms a smooth ball, stirring constantly with a wooden spoon. Remove from the heat and let cool for 5 minutes.

Add the eggs one at a time, beating well after each addition. Beat in the cheese and bacon. Drop by teaspoonfuls 2 inches apart onto a lightly greased baking sheet. Bake at 400 degrees for 20 to 25 minutes or until golden brown.
MAKES 5 dozen puffs

DEVILED CHEESE BALLS

6 ounces cream cheese, softened
4 ounces blue cheese, crumbled
2 (2-ounce) cans deviled ham
1/2 cup (or more) chopped pecans
1/2 small onion, finely chopped
1 cup finely chopped parsley
1 cup sour cream
1/4 teaspoon garlic salt
Pretzel sticks

Combine the cream cheese and blue cheese in a bowl and mix until blended. Stir in the ham, pecans and onion. Chill, covered, in the refrigerator. Shape into small balls and roll in the parsley. Arrange in a single layer on a serving platter and chill, covered, until serving time.

Combine the sour cream and garlic salt in a small bowl and chill, covered, in the refrigerator. Place in the center of the serving platter. Provide pretzel sticks as spears for the cheese balls. **SERVES 14 to 16**

BALSAMIC-GLAZED CHICKEN LEGS

1/2 cup good-quality balsamic vinegar
1/2 cup mold honey (clover or similar)
1/2 cup packed light brown sugar
1/4 cup soy sauce
5 garlic cloves, crushed
4 sprigs of rosemary
12 chicken legs
2 to 3 tablespoons sesame seeds

Combine the vinegar, honey, brown sugar, soy sauce, garlic and rosemary in a sealable plastic bag and seal tightly. Knead the bag until the brown sugar dissolves. Add the chicken legs to the bag and reseal. Marinate in the refrigerator for 2 to 3 hours, turning occasionally.

Drain the chicken, reserving the marinade. Arrange the chicken in a single layer on a baking sheet lined with foil. Bake at 450 degrees for 30 to 35 minutes or until the skin begins to caramelize and darken.

Bring the reserved marinade to a boil in a heavy saucepan and boil for 2 to 3 minutes, stirring constantly. Reduce the heat and cook over low to medium heat until thickened, stirring occasionally. Remove the chicken from the oven and baste with the thickened marinade using a pastry brush. Sprinkle with the sesame seeds and arrange on a serving platter. **SERVES 6 to 8**

Mahogany Chicken Wings

1¹/2 cups soy sauce
1 cup hoisin sauce
³/4 cup dry sherry
³/4 cup Chinese plum sauce
³/4 cup cider vinegar
¹/2 cup honey
18 green onions, minced
6 to 7 pounds chicken wings

Combine the soy sauce, hoisin sauce, sherry, plum sauce, vinegar, honey and green onions in a 3-quart saucepan and bring to a boil. Reduce the heat and simmer for 5 minutes. Let stand until cool. Pour the sauce over the chicken in a glass or plastic container, turning to coat. Marinate, covered, for 8 to 10 hours, turning occasionally.

Place the oven racks in the upper third and lower third of the oven. Drain the chicken, reserving the marinade. Arrange the chicken evenly in two oiled large shallow roasting pans.

Bake at 375 degrees for 1 to 1¹/2 hours, basting every 20 minutes with the reserved marinade and turning until evenly brown. Switch the pans halfway through the baking process. Remove the chicken to a sheet of foil to cool. Wrap the cooled chicken in foil and store in the refrigerator for up to 3 days. Serve at room temperature. **SERVES 20 to 24**

FRIED MOZZARELLA STICKS

1/2 cup all-purpose flour
1/8 to 1/4 teaspoon red pepper
2 eggs
1 tablespoon water
16 ounces mozzarella cheese sticks
1/2 cup seasoned bread crumbs
11/2 to 2 cups canola oil
Spaghetti sauce, heated

Mix the flour and red pepper together on a sheet of waxed paper. Whisk the eggs and water in a small bowl until blended. Coat the cheese sticks with the flour mixture, dip in the egg mixture and roll in the bread crumbs.

Pour enough canola oil into a skillet to measure 1/2 inch and heat to 375 degrees. Fry the cheese sticks in batches in a single layer in the hot oil just until the cheese begins to melt and the sticks are golden brown, turning once. Drain on paper towels and keep warm in a 200-degree oven. Serve with spaghetti sauce for dipping. **SERVES 6 to 8**

Parmesan Tuiles

¹/₂ cup (2 ounces) freshly shredded Parmesan cheese
  (medium-fine shreds)

Divide the cheese into twenty-four 1-teaspoon mounds on a nonstick baking sheet. Gently pat the mounds into 2-inch rounds of equal thickness.

Bake at 350 degrees for 5 minutes or until golden brown. Watch carefully as they burn quickly. Remove from the oven and let rest briefly on the baking sheet to firm. Lift the tuiles with a narrow spatula and place on a wire rack to cool. They will become crisp as they cool. Store in an airtight container.
Makes 24 tuiles

"The first thing I think of when you say 'Devon' is camaraderie and friendship."

—Beth Wright
  Chairman, Devon Country Fair

Parmesan Cheese Twists

1 sheet frozen puff pastry
1 egg
1 tablespoon water
¹/₄ cup (1 ounce) grated Parmesan cheese
¹/₂ teaspoon dried oregano, crushed
¹/₄ cup chopped fresh parsley

Thaw the pastry at room temperature for 30 minutes. Whisk the egg and water in a small bowl until blended. Mix the cheese, oregano and parsley in a small bowl. Unfold the pastry on a lightly floured surface and roll into a 10×14-inch rectangle. Cut lengthwise into halves.

Brush both halves of the pastry with the egg wash. Sprinkle the cheese mixture on one pastry half. Place the remaining pastry half egg side down over the cheese-topped half. Gently roll with a rolling pin to seal.

Cut the rectangle crosswise into twenty-eight ¹/₂-inch strips. Twist the strips and arrange 2 inches apart on a greased baking sheet, pressing down the ends. Brush the twists with the remaining egg wash. Bake at 400 degrees for 10 minutes or until golden brown. Serve warm or at room temperature. The crisps can be stored in an airtight container for up to 1 week. **MAKES 28 twists**

TO MAKE IN ADVANCE, TWIST THE PASTRY STRIPS AND ARRANGE ON A BAKING SHEET. BRUSH WITH THE EGG MIXTURE AND FREEZE. STORE THE FROZEN TWISTS IN A SEALABLE FREEZER BAG FOR UP TO 1 MONTH. BAKE THE FROZEN TWISTS ON A GREASED BAKING SHEET AT 400 DEGREES FOR 15 MINUTES OR UNTIL GOLDEN BROWN.

SAVORY SABLÉS

1³/4 cups all-purpose flour
1¹/2 cups (3 sticks) butter, chilled
8 ounces Gruyère cheese, coarsely shredded
¹/4 teaspoon cayenne pepper
¹/4 teaspoon dry mustard
1 egg yolk
1 tablespoon water

Combine the flour, butter, cheese, cayenne pepper and dry mustard in
a food processor. Pulse until the mixture forms a ball, adding cold water
1 teaspoon at a time if needed.

Roll the pastry ¹/4 inch thick on a lightly floured surface. Cut into
decorative shapes such as stars or half-moons. Arrange ³/4 inches apart on two
parchment-lined baking sheets. Brush with a mixture of the egg yolk and
1 tablespoon water.

Chill for 30 minutes or until firm. Bake at 350 degrees for 10 minutes
or until golden brown. Let cool on the baking sheets for 2 minutes and remove
to a wire rack. Serve warm or at room temperature. **MAKES 40 sablés**

PREPARE SABLÉS UP TO TWO WEEKS IN ADVANCE AND STORE IN AN AIRTIGHT
CONTAINER AT ROOM TEMPERATURE. MAKE SPICY SABLES BY ADDING 2 TEASPOONS
PAPRIKA TO THE FLOUR MIXTURE. OR, OMIT THE DRY MUSTARD AND ADD
2 TEASPOONS CARAWAY SEEDS TO THE FLOUR MIXTURE FOR A DIFFERENT FLAVOR.
SERVE WITH DIPS, SOUPS OR BY THEMSELVES.

Bloody Marys on a Stick

2 small containers ripe cherry tomatoes
$^1/_2$ (750-milliliter) bottle good-quality vodka
1 teaspoon sea salt, or to taste
1 teaspoon cumin, or to taste

Pierce each tomato in places with a wooden pick. Combine the tomatoes and vodka in a large bowl and mix well. Stir in the salt and cumin. Marinate for several hours, or for the best flavor marinate 8 to 10 hours. Drain, reserving the liquid for "real" Bloody Marys.

Serve in a large bowl with wooden skewers. Place small bowls of sea salt and cumin by the tomatoes for additional dipping. **SERVES 10 to 12**

THESE ARE VERY REFRESHING AND GREAT FOR A SUMMER PARTY. ADD HOT SAUCE AND RED PEPPER FLAKES FOR A SPICIER FLAVOR, OR USE YOUR IMAGINATION AND ADD ADDITIONAL SPICES ACCORDING TO TASTE.

COCKTAIL CAULIFLOWER

1 head cauliflower
2 eggs, lightly beaten
2 cups cornflake crumbs

Separate the cauliflower into florets, discarding the stems. Dip the florets in the eggs and coat with the crumbs. Arrange the coated florets on a lightly greased baking sheet. Bake at 350 degrees for 20 minutes or until crisp. Serve immediately. **SERVES 8 to 10**

ROASTED FIGS IN PORT

1 or 2 packages ripe figs
1 (750-milliliter) good-quality port
  (Nor Ruby preferred)

Cut the figs into halves and arrange cut sides down in a baking dish. Pour the wine over the figs until one-fourth of the surface of the figs is covered.

Bake at 350 degrees for 20 minutes. Let stand until cool. Serve with your choice of cheese; soft goat cheese goes very well. **SERVES 6 to 8**

GRILLED FIGS

6 figs, cut into halves
1/4 cup (1 ounce) crumbled Gorgonzola cheese
6 slices prosciutto, cut into halves

Arrange the figs cut side up on a baking sheet. Sprinkle each half with
1 teaspoon of the cheese and wrap with one-half slice of the prosciutto.
Broil until the cheese melts and the prosciutto is sizzling. Prepare on the grill,
if desired. **SERVES 4 to 6**

SERVE THESE AS AN HORS D'OEUVRE OR ALONGSIDE A SALAD TOSSED WITH
BALSAMIC VINAIGRETTE.

Greg Landis Famous Homemade Hot Peppers

Fresh long hot red Italian peppers
Extra-virgin olive oil

Slice the peppers into halves and remove all the seeds. Carefully remove the inner white veins. Arrange the peppers in a shallow dish and add enough olive oil to cover, turning to coat. Marinate for 24 hours, turning occasionally; drain.

Arrange the peppers on a baking sheet and roast at 350 degrees for 2 hours, turning every 30 minutes. Immediately remove to a shallow dish and chill. Serve as needed. **Makes a variable amount**

Jicama Appetizer

Jicama
Lime juice
Chopped red bell pepper
Salt and pepper to taste

Peel and cut the jicama into 1/4-inch strips. Arrange the jicama in a shallow dish and drizzle with lime juice to prevent browning and for flavor. Sprinkle with bell pepper and season with salt and pepper. **Makes a variable amount**

Hot Cheese and Olive Puffs

48 small pimento-stuffed green olives
1 cup sifted all-purpose flour
1 teaspoon paprika
1/2 teaspoon salt
Cayenne pepper to taste
8 ounces sharp Cheddar cheese, shredded
1/2 cup (1 stick) butter, softened

Drain the olives on paper towels. Sift the flour, paprika, salt and cayenne pepper together. Mix the cheese and butter in a bowl until combined. Add the flour mixture and mix well.

Wrap each olive with approximately 1 teaspoon of the dough and seal. Freeze at this point for future use, if desired.

Arrange the wrapped olives on an ungreased baking sheet. Bake at 400 degrees for 15 minutes. If frozen, bake for 20 minutes. Serve warm or at room temperature. **Makes 4 dozen puffs**

For variety, substitute small cocktail onions for the olives.

MARINATED OLIVES

3½ cups (with or without pits) assorted
*   black and green olives, drained*
Zest of 1 lemon, cut into small strips
3 large garlic cloves, slivered
3 tablespoons crushed fresh rosemary
½ to 1 teaspoon red pepper flakes
Sea salt to taste
Olive oil

Toss the olives, lemon zest, garlic, rosemary, red pepper flakes and salt in a bowl. Add enough olive oil to generously coat and toss. Marinate, covered, in the refrigerator for 8 to 10 hours, stirring occasionally. To intensify the flavor, marinate for several weeks. **SERVES 10 to 12**

STUFFED OLIVES

1/3 cup minced parsley
2 tablespoons olive oil
1 garlic clove, minced
1 (6-ounce) can extra-large or
*   colossal pitted black olives*
1 (2-ounce) can flat anchovy fillets,
*   drained and cut into halves*
10 or 12 cherry tomatoes, stems removed

Mix the parsley, olive oil and garlic in a medium bowl. Stuff each olive with an anchovy half. Add the stuffed olives to the parsley mixture and toss to coat. Let stand at room temperature for 1 hour and stir in the tomatoes. Or, marinate in the refrigerator for 8 to 10 hours. Bring to room temperature before serving and stir in the tomatoes. SERVES **10 to 12**

SUN-DRIED TOMATOES AND ARTICHOKES

2 (14-ounce) cans artichoke bottoms, drained
2 tablespoons lemon juice
8 sun-dried tomatoes, sliced
12 (cherry-tomato-size) mozzarella balls
$1/3$ cup pesto sauce

Rinse the artichoke bottoms in cold water and drain. Toss with the lemon juice in a bowl to prevent discoloration. Let stand for 5 minutes. Trim the bottoms to allow the artichokes to stand upright.

Arrange the artichokes upright on a baking sheet lined with baking parchment. Top each with one sun-dried tomato slice, one mozzarella ball and one teaspoon of the pesto. Roast at 400 degrees for 5 minutes. Serve immediately.
SERVES 8 to 10

SPINACH AND CHEESE BITES

2 (10-ounce) packages frozen chopped spinach,
 thawed and drained
1/4 cup (1/2 stick) butter
1 cup all-purpose flour
1 teaspoon baking powder
Salt and pepper to taste
1 cup milk
3 eggs, beaten
4 cups (16 ounces) shredded Monterey Jack cheese,
 Cheddar cheese or a combination of the two
1 tablespoon minced onion

Press the excess moisture from the spinach. Melt the butter in a 9×13-inch baking dish, tilting the dish to cover evenly. Mix the flour, baking powder, salt and pepper together. Whisk the milk and eggs in a bowl until blended. Add the dry ingredients and mix well. Stir in the spinach, cheese and onion.

Pour into the prepared baking dish. Bake at 350 degrees for 35 minutes. Let cool in the pan on a wire rack for 1 hour or longer. Cut into bite-size pieces to serve. May be frozen at this point in sealable plastic bags for future use. Reheat at 325 degrees for 10 minutes. **MAKES 40 to 45 bites**

SPICED ALMONDS

¹/4 cup sugar
¹/4 cup sesame seeds
2 teaspoons ground ginger
1 teaspoon salt
1 teaspoon crushed red pepper
¹/2 teaspoon ground cumin
2 tablespoons vegetable oil
3 cups blanched whole almonds
¹/2 cup sugar

Combine ¹/4 cup sugar, the sesame seeds, ginger, salt, red pepper and cumin in a large bowl and mix well. Heat the oil in a skillet over medium heat and add the almonds. Cook for about 2 minutes or until the almonds are fragrant, stirring constantly. Sprinkle with ¹/2 cup sugar and continue to cook, shaking the skillet occasionally to prevent the almonds from burning. Stir only when the almonds are golden, smoking slightly and the sugar has begun to melt and caramelize.

Remove from the heat. Add the almonds to the sesame seed mixture and toss quickly to coat. Spread in a single layer on a nonstick baking sheet and use two forks to separate the almonds while hot. Let stand until cool and separate by hand. Store in an airtight container. SERVES **10 to 12**

Rosemary Cashews

1 pound cashews
3 tablespoons chopped rosemary leaves
1 1/2 tablespoons butter, melted
1 tablespoon light brown sugar
1 tablespoon kosher salt
1/2 teaspoon cayenne pepper

Spread the cashews in a single layer on a rimmed baking sheet. Bake at 350 degrees for 5 to 8 minutes or until the cashews are fragrant and lightly toasted.

Combine the rosemary, butter, brown sugar, salt and cayenne pepper in a bowl and mix well. Add the warm cashews and toss to coat. Serve warm, if possible. SERVES **8 to 10**

GLAZED PECANS

1/2 cup sugar
1/4 cup water
2 teaspoons unsweetened baking cocoa
1/2 teaspoon ground cinnamon
Pinch of salt
3 cups unsalted pecan halves

Combine the sugar, water, baking cocoa, cinnamon and salt in a saucepan and mix well. Cook over high heat until blended. Stir in the pecans and bring to a boil. Remove from the heat.

Toss and stir constantly for 3 to 5 minutes or until the syrup thickens and the pecans are coated. Spread the pecans on a sheet of waxed paper; do not allow to touch. Let stand until cool. Store in an airtight container.
MAKES about 12 (1/4-cup) servings

CANDIED WALNUTS

6 tablespoons sugar
3 tablespoons orange juice
2 cups walnut halves

Line a baking sheet with foil and spray with nonstick cooking spray. Mix the sugar and orange juice in a 10-inch skillet. Cook over medium heat until the sugar dissolves and the mixture is simmering. Stir in the walnuts and toss to coat.

Cook for 2 minutes longer, stirring constantly. Spread in a single layer on the prepared baking sheet. Bake at 375 degrees for 6 to 7 minutes or until the walnuts are fragrant and lightly toasted. Let stand until cool and break up any large pieces. **SERVES 12 to 14**

HERBED WALNUTS

2 tablespoons olive oil
2 tablespoons butter
1 pound walnut halves
1 tablespoon dried rosemary
2 teaspoons salt
1 teaspoon paprika

Heat the olive oil and butter in a roasting pan in a 325-degree oven until the butter melts. Maintain the oven temperature. Add the walnuts and stir to coat.

Spread the walnuts in a single layer over the bottom of the roasting pan and sprinkle with the rosemary, salt and paprika. Bake for 20 to 25 minutes or until the walnuts are fragrant and lightly toasted, stirring several times.
SERVES **12 to 14**

UNION SQUARE CAFÉ BAR NUTS

1 pound assorted unsalted nuts
2 tablespoons coarsely chopped rosemary
1 tablespoon unsalted butter, melted
2 teaspoons brown sugar
2 teaspoons ground sea salt
1/2 to 1 teaspoon cayenne pepper, or to taste

Spread the nuts on a baking sheet and bake at 355 degrees for 5 to 10 minutes or until the nuts are fragrant and lightly toasted. Combine the rosemary, butter, brown sugar, salt and cayenne pepper in a large bowl and mix well. Add the warm nuts and toss to coat. Serve warm for the best flavor.
SERVES **10 to 12**

Canapés, Crostini and Sandwiches

Famous horses in the stables have included Grand Prix jumpers Idle Dice and Number One Spy, both owned by Harry Gill, as well as Olympic jumper Gem Twist. Famous American Saddlebreds have included World Champion Sky Watch, among many other top horses.

Grand Prix

Champagne Cup

Chesapeake City Crab Soup

Sun-Dried Tomato Pâté

Grand Prix Beer Cheese Spread

Roasted Bell Pepper
and Olive Crostini

CRAB TRIANGLES

4 English muffins
1½ cups (6 ounces) shredded sharp Cheddar cheese
7 tablespoons margarine, softened
2 tablespoons mayonnaise
1 garlic clove, minced
1 teaspoon Old Bay seasoning (optional)
8 ounces crab meat, drained and flaked

Split the muffins into halves. Combine the cheese, margarine, mayonnaise, garlic and Old Bay seasoning in a bowl and mix well. Fold in the crab meat.

Spread the crab meat mixture on the cut sides of the muffins and cut each half into six wedges. Arrange the wedges in a single layer on a baking sheet. Bake at 400 degrees for 10 minutes. Serve warm. **MAKES 4 dozen triangles**

THIS RECIPE DOUBLES WELL. YOU CAN ALSO SPREAD THE CRAB MEAT MIXTURE ON THE CUT SIDES OF THE MUFFIN HALVES AND FREEZE. STORE IN SEALABLE PLASTIC FREEZER BAGS. THAW IN THE REFRIGERATOR AND CUT THE HALVES INTO WEDGES BEFORE BAKING.

CRABBY CHEESE CANAPÉS

2 loaves fresh white bread,
  crusts trimmed
1/4 cup (1/2 stick) butter
1/4 cup all-purpose flour
1/2 cup milk
2 cups crab meat, shells removed
1 teaspoon Worcestershire sauce
1/2 teaspoon dry mustard
Salt and pepper to taste
Tabasco sauce to taste

1 1/2 cups (6 ounces) shredded
  Cheddar cheese
1/4 cup heavy cream
2 tablespoons butter, softened
1 teaspoon Worcestershire sauce
1/2 teaspoon dry mustard
1/4 teaspoon salt
1/4 teaspoon paprika
1 egg

Cut the bread slices into desired shapes and arrange on a baking sheet. Toast at 350 degrees on one side until light brown.

Melt 1/4 cup butter in a saucepan and stir in the flour. Cook until blended, stirring constantly. Add the milk gradualy and stir until combined. Mix in the crab meat. Add 1 teaspoon Worcestershire sauce, 1/2 teaspoon dry mustard, salt to taste, pepper and Tabasco sauce and mix well. Simmer for 2 minutes, stirring frequently. Let stand until cool.

Beat the cheese, cream and 2 tablespoons butter in a mixing bowl until creamed. Beat in 1 teaspoon Worcestershire sauce, 1/2 teaspoon dry mustard, 1/4 teaspoon salt and the paprika. Add the egg and beat until fluffy.

Spread the crab meat mixture on the untoasted side of the bread shapes and top each with a dollop of the cheese mixture. Arrange in a single layer on a baking sheet and freeze. Thaw in the refrigerator just before serving and arrange in a single layer on a baking sheet. Broil until light brown and bubbly.
MAKES 6 dozen canapés

MANGO CRAB STACKS

BRIOCHE ROUNDS
1 (1-pound) loaf brioche
2 tablespoons butter

CRAB STACKS
1/3 cup plus 3 tablespoons
   mayonnaise
1 3/4 teaspoons wasabi paste
6 ounces lump crab meat,
   drained and flaked

1 small red bell pepper,
   cut into 1/4-inch pieces
   (1/2 cup)
2 tablespoons chopped
   fresh cilantro
2 tablespoons fresh lemon juice
Kosher salt to taste
3 ripe large mangoes, cut into
   1/4-inch slices

To prepare the rounds, cut the loaf into 3/4-inch-thick slices. Using a 1 1/2-inch cutter, cut thirty-six rounds from the slices. Melt 1 tablespoon of the butter in a 12-inch skillet over medium heat. Add half the rounds and cook for 1 to 2 minutes per side or until golden brown. Remove to a wire rack to cool. Repeat the process with the remaining butter and rounds. Store in an airtight container at room temperature for up to 2 days.

To prepare the stacks, combine the mayonnaise and wasabi paste in a bowl and mix well. Remove 1/4 cup of the mixture to a separate bowl and reserve. Add the crab meat, bell pepper, cilantro and lemon juice to the remaining mayonnaise mixture and mix well. Season with salt. Chill, tightly covered with plastic wrap, in the refrigerator.

Cut thirty-six rounds from the mango slices using a 1 1/2-inch cutter. Chop the leftover pieces of mango for garnish. Spread some of the reserved wasabi mayonnaise on each slice of the brioche and layer each with one mango round. Top with 1 teaspoon of the crab meat mixture and garnish with the chopped mango. Serve immediately. **MAKES 3 dozen crab stacks**

YOU MAY MAKE WASABI PASTE BY MIXING 2 1/2 TEASPOONS WASABI POWDER WITH ABOUT 1 1/4 TEASPOONS WATER, IF DESIRED.

BAKED OYSTERS

OYSTER SAUCE
1 cup mayonnaise
1/4 cup chili sauce
2 tablespoons lemon juice
1/2 teaspoon paprika
3 dashes of Tabasco sauce
Salt and pepper to taste
Old Bay seasoning to taste

OYSTERS
2 pounds frozen chopped spinach, cooked and drained
24 large oysters, shelled
Bacon bits to taste
Grated Parmesan cheese to taste
Paprika to taste

To prepare the sauce, combine the mayonnaise, chili sauce, lemon juice, paprika, Tabasco sauce, salt, pepper and Old Bay seasoning in a bowl and mix well.

To prepare the oysters, press the excess moisture from the spinach. Grease a 2-quart baking dish or individual ramekins. Layer the oysters, oyster sauce, spinach and bacon bits. Sprinkle with Parmesan cheese and paprika. Bake at 375 degrees for 12 to 15 minutes or until the cheese browns and begins to bubble. Serve with baguette slices. **SERVES 10 to 12**

SHRIMP ZUCCHINI ROUNDS

1 (16-ounce) package frozen deveined peeled shrimp
1 cup mayonnaise
1 tablespoon dill weed
1/4 teaspoon salt
6 small zucchini

Cook the shrimp using package directions early on the day of serving. Place the shrimp in a medium bowl and chill, covered, in the refrigerator.

Combine the mayonnaise, dill weed and salt in a bowl 30 minutes before serving. Cut the zucchini diagonally into 1/4-inch rounds. Spoon about 1/2 teaspoon of the mayonnaise mixture onto each zucchini round and top each with one shrimp. Garnish with capers. **MAKES about 40 rounds**

CHARLESTON CANAPÉ

8 ounces cream cheese, softened
1 (12-ounce) jar cocktail sauce
8 ounces fresh shrimp, cooked, peeled, deveined and
    cut into small pieces
4 ounces Monterey Jack cheese, shredded
6 green onions with tops, trimmed and chopped
1/2 red bell pepper or green bell pepper, chopped
1/2 cup chopped black olives

Spread the cream cheese over the bottom of a deep plate or quiche dish. Layer with the cocktail sauce, shrimp, cheese, green onions, bell pepper and olives in the order listed. Serve with melba rounds and/or assorted party crackers. **SERVES 10 to 12**

CRAB MEAT MAY BE SUBSTITUTED FOR THE SHRIMP.

SEVEN-LAYER SALMON BITES

10 ounces cream cheese, softened
2 teaspoons fresh lemon juice
1 teaspoon finely grated lemon zest
3/4 teaspoon finely chopped chives
1/4 teaspoon salt
1/4 teaspoon pepper
6 (5×6-inch) oval slices dark pumpernickel
    sandwich bread (about 1/2 inch thick)
4 ounces thinly sliced smoked Scottish salmon
1/4 cup (2 ounces) salmon roe

Combine the cream cheese, lemon juice, lemon zest, chives, salt and pepper in a small bowl and mix well.

Stack the bread slices and trim to 3¹/₄×4¹/₄-inch rectangles. Spread each bread rectangle with 1 heaping tablespoon of the cream cheese mixture and top with a thin layer of the salmon; cut the salmon with kitchen shears to fit the bread slices. Continue layering each with 1 heaping tablespoon of the remaining cream cheese mixture and another thin layer of the remaining salmon. Spread with the remaining cream cheese mixture. Trim the edges of the rectangles to make uniform and arrange on a platter.

Chill for 1 hour or until the tops are firm. Cut the rectangles into eight 1×1¹/₂-inch pieces. Top each piece with a rounded ¹/₄ teaspoon of the roe.
MAKES 48 bites

CURRIED TUNA CANAPÉS

1/2 cup mayonnaise
1/4 cup fresh parsley, minced
2 tablespoons Major Grey's chutney, chopped
1 tablespoon red wine vinegar
1/4 teaspoon curry powder
1 (7-ounce) can water-pack tuna, drained and flaked
1/4 cup currants, chopped
1/4 cup pecans, toasted and chopped
Sliced cucumbers or baked miniature tart shells

Combine the mayonnaise, parsley, chutney, vinegar and curry powder in a bowl and mix well. Stir in the tuna. Add the currants and pecans and mix well.

Spoon onto cucumber slices or into tart shells. Serve immediately.

SERVES 6 to 8

EVERY TIME THESE CANAPÉS ARE SERVED, THE PLATTER IS EMPTIED QUICKLY.

SAUSAGE SNACKS

1 to 2 pounds bulk pork sausage
1 large onion, chopped
2 cups baking mix
3/4 cup milk
1 egg, lightly beaten
1 tablespoon caraway seeds or poppy seeds
1 1/2 cups sour cream
1 egg, lightly beaten
1/4 teaspoon salt
Paprika to taste

Brown the sausage with the onion in a skillet, stirring until the sausage is crumbly; drain. Combine the baking mix, milk and one egg in a bowl and mix well. Spread in a greased 10×15-inch baking pan. Sprinkle with the caraway seeds and top with the sausage mixture.

Combine the sour cream, one egg and the salt in a bowl and mix well. Spread evenly over the prepared layers and sprinkle with paprika. Bake at 350 degrees for 25 to 30 minutes or until set. Cut into rectangles. Serve warm.
SERVES 6 to 8

Bacon and Cheese Frittata

1 tablespoon olive oil or bacon grease
1$^1/_2$ cups finely chopped onions
$^1/_4$ teaspoon kosher salt
$^1/_8$ teaspoon pepper
5 eggs, beaten
1 cup chopped crisp-cooked bacon
$^3/_4$ cup (3 ounces) grated Swiss or Gruyère cheese
$^1/_3$ cup cream
$^1/_4$ cup dry bread crumbs
2 tablespoons chopped fresh chives
1 teaspoon chopped fresh rosemary
$^1/_8$ teaspoon pepper
1 tablespoon chopped fresh chives

Heat the olive oil in a nonstick skillet over medium heat and add the onions, salt and $^1/_8$ teaspoon pepper. Cook for 6 to 8 minutes or until the onions are tender. Combine with the eggs, bacon, cheese, cream, bread crumbs, 2 tablespoons chives, the rosemary and $^1/_8$ teaspoon pepper in a bowl and mix well.

Pour into a buttered and floured 8×8-inch baking dish and sprinkle with 1 tablespoon chives. Bake at 325 degrees for 35 to 45 minutes or until set. Cool in pan on a wire rack. Trim the outside edges and cut into squares. Arrange on a baking sheet and reheat, covered with foil, until warm. **Makes 30 to 34 squares**

FOR VARIETY, SUBSTITUTE HAM FOR THE BACON. THIS IS GOOD SERVED THE SECOND DAY.

DEVON TURF CLUB DELIGHTS

8 ounces Velveeta cheese
1 white onion
1 (12-ounce) can Spam, finely chopped
60 Triscuits

Freeze the cheese for 1 hour and shred. Grate the onion on the finest side of the grater over a mixing bowl, allowing the juices to drain into the bowl. Stir in the cheese and Spam.

Spoon onto the crackers and arrange in a single layer on a baking sheet. Broil for 1 minute or until golden brown and bubbly. **MAKES 5 dozen delights**

A FOND MEMORY . . . "WINNING THE PAIR CHILD EVENT AT DEVON WITH MY DAUGHTER, FRANNY ABBOTT, AND HAVING A BIG SHOT OF VODKA BEFORE GOING INTO THE RING."

—BETTY MORAN

Blue Cheese Puffs

¹/₂ cup (1 stick) butter
8 ounces blue cheese, crumbled
1 (10-count) can refrigerator biscuits

Combine the butter and cheese in a saucepan and cook over low heat until blended. Cut the biscuits into quarters. Arrange 2 inches apart on a baking sheet. Pour the cheese mixture over the biscuits. Bake at 350 degrees for 10 minutes or until brown. **Serves 10 to 12**

Brie Soufflé

¹/₂ cup (1 stick) unsalted butter, softened
8 slices white bread, crusts trimmed
16 ounces (not fully aged) Brie cheese,
*   rind removed and cheese cut into cubes*
2 cups half-and-half
1 tablespoon chopped fresh dill weed
1 teaspoon salt
Dash of Tabasco sauce
4 eggs

Spread the butter on one side of each slice of bread. Arrange half the slices butter side up over the bottom of a buttered 1¹/₂-quart soufflé dish. Sprinkle with half the Brie. Top with the remaining bread and remaining Brie. The soufflé may be covered and chilled for up to 24 hours at this point.

Whisk the half-and-half, dill weed, salt, Tabasco sauce and eggs in a bowl until blended 1 hour before serving. Pour over the prepared layers and let stand at room temperature for 30 minutes. Bake at 350 degrees for 30 minutes or until bubbly and golden brown. Serve immediately. **Serves 6 to 8**

CHIVE BREAD WITH RADISHES

1 loaf Italian bread
$1/2$ cup (1 stick) butter, softened
1 bunch radishes, trimmed and cut into paper-thin slices
1 bunch chives, trimmed and finely chopped
Freshly ground pepper to taste

Cut the bread into $1/2$-inch rounds. Spread the butter on one side of each of the rounds. Top the buttered rounds with the radish slices and press gently. Sprinkle generously with the chives and press gently. Season with pepper. Arrange on a serving platter and serve with a good German beer.
SERVES 24 to 25 depending on the size of the bread loaf

Parmesan Onion Puffs

10 slices firm white bread
1/2 cup mayonnaise
2 ounces Parmigiano-Reggiano cheese, finely grated
1 tablespoon minced onion
1/4 teaspoon cayenne pepper

Cut four rounds from each bread slice using a cutter. Arrange the rounds on a baking sheet. Place the baking sheet on the oven rack in the upper third of the oven. Toast at 400 degrees for 3 to 4 minutes or until light brown. Cool the toasts slightly on the baking sheet on a rack. Maintain the oven temperature.

Combine the mayonnaise, cheese, onion and cayenne pepper in a bowl and mix well. Top each toast with a rounded 1/2 teaspoon of the cheese mixture, spreading to the edges. Bake for 6 minutes or until puffed and golden brown.
Makes 40 puffs

Grilled Polenta Rounds

1 (18-ounce) roll plain polenta or sun-dried tomato polenta,
   cut into $1/2$-inch slices
$1/4$ cup extra-virgin olive oil
1 (16-ounce) jar roasted red peppers, drained
$1/2$ cup pitted kalamata olives
$1/2$ cup flat-leaf parsley leaves
$1/4$ cup coarsely chopped red onion
2 tablespoons drained capers
1 or 2 garlic cloves
$1/2$ teaspoon red pepper flakes

Brush both sides of the polenta slices lightly with the olive oil. Grill over high heat or in a grill pan over high heat for 2 to 3 minutes on each side.

Combine the roasted peppers, olives, parsley, onion, capers, garlic and red pepper flakes in a food processor. Pulse until chopped and combined. Top the grilled polenta slices evenly with the salsa and arrange on a serving platter. Serve immediately. SERVES 12 to 15

SUBSTITUTE ANY OF YOUR FAVORITE SALSAS FOR THE ROASTED RED PEPPER SALSA.

Parmesan Pita Crisps

4 (6-inch) pita rounds, split
6 tablespoons olive oil
1 teaspoon dried whole oregano leaves
1 teaspoon garlic powder
1/2 cup (2 ounces) grated Parmesan cheese
1 1/2 tablespoons sesame seeds

Cut each pita round into six wedges. Arrange the wedges cut side up on an ungreased baking sheet. Mix the olive oil, oregano and garlic powder in a bowl and brush the wedges lightly with the mixture.

Mix the cheese and sesame seeds in a bowl and sprinkle over the top of the wedges. Bake at 425 degrees for 10 minutes or until light brown. Remove to a wire rack to cool. Store in an airtight container. **MAKES 4 dozen crisps**

SHIITAKE AND BRIE PIZZA

3 ounces shiitake mushrooms
2 tablespoons butter
1/4 teaspoon crushed garlic
4 (6- to 7-inch) flour tortillas
4 ounces Brie cheese, thinly sliced
1 cup chopped fresh plum tomatoes
1/3 cup thinly sliced scallions or green onions

Remove the stems from the mushrooms and discard or save for use in stews or to flavor broths. Thinly slice the caps. Melt the butter in a small saucepan and add the garlic. Cook for 30 seconds, stirring constantly. Remove from the heat.

Arrange the tortillas in a single layer on a baking sheet. Cover the tortillas with the sliced cheese and sprinkle evenly with the tomatoes, mushrooms and scallions. Drizzle with the garlic butter. Bake at 350 degrees for 10 minutes or until the cheese melts and the mushrooms are tender. Cut each tortilla into four wedges, if desired. **MAKES 16 wedges**

White Cocktail Pizza

Vegetable oil
Cornmeal
Thawed frozen pizza dough or refrigerator pizza dough
1 garlic clove
3 tablespoons olive oil
3 tablespoons chopped fresh rosemary
Fresh sage leaves to taste
¼ cup grated locatelli cheese

Coat a large pizza pan with vegetable oil and sprinkle with corn meal. Stretch the dough into a large circle and place onto the prepared pizza pan. Rub the garlic clove over the dough and drizzle with the olive oil. Or, drizzle with garlic oil. Sprinkle with the rosemary and arrange the sage leaves over the top. Sprinkle with the cheese.

Bake at 400 degrees for about 20 minutes or until light brown and bubbly. Cool slightly and cut into wedges with scissors or a pizza cutter. **Serves 6 to 8**

Pizzazz

1 cup oil-pack sun-dried tomatoes or
*   roasted cherry tomatoes, drained and julienned*
4 teaspoons balsamic vinegar
Pinch of pepper
5 large garlic bulbs
2 tablespoons olive oil
6 English muffins, cut into halves
3/4 cup (3 ounces) crumbled Cambozola, at room temperature
1/2 cup julienned fresh basil

Combine the tomatoes, vinegar and pepper in a bowl and mix well. Marinate at room temperature, stirring occasionally.

Make a horizontal cut about 1 inch below the top of each garlic bulb and set the tops back on the bulbs. Place the garlic bulbs on a large piece of foil and brush the garlic with the olive oil. Fold the foil over to seal and place the pouch on a baking sheet. Bake at 350 degrees for 1 hour or until the garlic is light brown and tender. Let stand until cool. Remove the garlic pulp from the skins by squeezing from the bottom of each clove and place in a bowl. Mash the pulp with the back of a spoon until smooth.

Increase the oven temperature to 375 degrees. Spread 1 1/2 teaspoons of the garlic over each muffin half. Spread 1 tablespoon of the cheese and 1 tablespoon of the tomato mixture evenly over the garlic on each muffin half. Arrange the muffin halves on a baking sheet lined with foil and place on the bottom oven rack. Bake for 12 minutes or until the cheese melts and the pizzazz are crisp. Remove from the oven and sprinkle with the basil. Cut each half into four wedges. Serve immediately. **Makes 4 dozen pizzazz**

The garlic mixture can be prepared up to 1 week in advance and stored, covered, in the refrigerator. Bring to room temperature before using. Assemble up to 3 hours in advance of serving.

Bruschetta Two Ways

1 French bread baguette, cut into 1/2-inch slices
    (about 24 slices)
2 small red bell peppers, each cut into 6 strips
1 cup fresh ricotta cheese
2 tablespoons extra-virgin olive oil
2 tablespoons chopped fresh oregano
1/2 teaspoon salt
Freshly ground pepper to taste
3 vine-ripe tomatoes, seeded and chopped
2 garlic cloves, minced
1 tablespoon sugar
6 fresh basil leaves, torn
1 teaspoon salt
Olive oil for drizzling

Lightly char the bread slices on both sides over hot coals, turning halfway through the grilling process. Roast the bell peppers over hot coals. Combine the ricotta cheese, 2 tablespoons olive oil, the oregano, 1/2 teaspoon salt and pepper in a bowl and mix well. Spread on half the toast and top each with a strip of roasted red pepper.

Combine the tomatoes, garlic, sugar, basil and 1 teaspoon salt in a bowl and mix well. Spoon on the remaining toast. Arrange both varieties of the bruschetta on a serving platter and drizzle with olive oil. Serve immediately.
Makes 2 dozen bruschetta

DEVON TURF CLUB CROSTINI

1 pound ground beef
Italian seasoning to taste
Salt and pepper to taste
Garlic powder to taste
Oregano to taste
Basil to taste
1 cup olive oil
¹/₂ cup red vinegar
¹/₂ cup (1 stick) butter
3 tablespoons minced garlic
6 to 8 crusty hoagie rolls
8 ounces provolone cheese, sliced or cut into chunks

Brown the ground beef with the Italian seasoning, salt, pepper, garlic powder, oregano and basil in a skillet, stirring until the ground beef is crumbly; drain. Bring the olive oil, vinegar, butter and garlic to a simmer in a 2- or 3-quart saucepan.

Fill the hoagie rolls evenly with the ground beef mixture and drizzle with the vinegar mixture. Top with the cheese. Arrange the rolls on a baking sheet and broil for 1 to 2 minutes or until the cheese melts. Cut each roll into three or four servings. Serve immediately. SERVES **18 to 24**

Roasted Bell Pepper and Olive Crostini

2 large red bell peppers,
*   cut lengthwise into halves*
2 large yellow bell peppers,
*   cut lengthwise into halves*
1/2 cup sliced green olives
1/2 cup sliced black olives
1 tablespoon drained capers
1 teaspoon olive oil
32 (1/2-inch-thick) diagonal slices
*   French bread baguette*

Arrange the bell peppers skin side up on a baking sheet lined with foil; flatten with the palm of hand. Broil 3 inches from the heat source for 12 minutes or until blackened and charred. Place the roasted peppers in a sealable plastic bag and seal tightly. Let stand for 15 minutes. Peel and discard the skins. Cut the roasted peppers into thin julienne strips.

Combine with the olives, capers and olive oil in a bowl and mix well. Let stand at room temperature for 2 hours, stirring occasionally. Spoon about 1 tablespoon of the mixture on each baguette slice. **MAKES 32 crostini**

EYE-OF-ROUND ROAST WITH HORSERADISH

EYE-OF-ROUND ROAST
1 cup soy sauce
1/2 cup vegetable oil
1/4 cup gin
3 garlic cloves, crushed
1 (4-pound) eye-of-round roast

HORSERADISH SAUCE
1 cup heavy whipping cream
1 cup mayonnaise
Pinch of salt
1/4 cup horseradish, or to taste

To prepare the roast, combine the soy sauce, oil, gin and garlic in a shallow dish. Add the roast and turn to coat. Marinate, covered with plastic wrap, in the refrigerator for 24 to 48 hours, turning three or four times; drain. Pat the roast dry with paper towels.

Place the roast in a baking pan and roast at 350 degrees for about 1 hour for medium-rare, or to the desired degree of doneness. Let cool slightly and chill in the refrigerator; thinly slice.

To prepare the sauce, beat the whipping cream in a mixing bowl until soft peaks form. Add the mayonnaise and salt and beat until blended. Fold in the horseradish. Serve the roast with Parker House rolls. **SERVES 30 to 40**

FOR A LIGHTER HORSERADISH SAUCE, OMIT THE MAYONNAISE.

Fillet Tartare

1 pound freshly ground beef tenderloin fillet tips
1/2 onion, finely chopped
1 egg, lightly beaten
1 tablespoon Champagne mustard
*   (Cherchies preferred)*
1 tablespoon olive oil
1 tablespoon aged balsamic vinegar
1 teaspoon sherry pepper sauce
*   (Outerbridge preferred) (optional)*
1 garlic clove, minced
1 loaf cocktail pumpernickel bread

Combine the ground beef, onion, egg, Champagne mustard, olive oil, vinegar, pepper sauce and garlic in a bowl and mix well. Chill, covered, in the refrigerator. Serve on the bread slices. **Serves 6 to 8**

IF YOU ARE CONCERNED ABOUT USING RAW EGG YOLKS, USE YOLKS FROM EGGS PASTEURIZED IN THEIR SHELLS, WHICH ARE SOLD AT SOME SPECIALTY FOOD STORES, OR USE AN EQUIVALENT AMOUNT OF PASTEURIZED EGG SUBSTITUTE.

COCKTAIL REUBENS

Thousand Island salad dressing
36 slices party rye
1 or 2 packages sliced corned beef
1 (15-ounce) can sauerkraut, drained
36 slices Swiss cheese

Spread the salad dressing on one side of each bread slice. Arrange the slices dressing side up in a single layer on a baking sheet. Layer each with one slice of folded corned beef, some of the sauerkraut and one slice of the cheese. Bake at 400 degrees for 5 minutes or until the cheese melts. Serve immediately.
MAKES 3 dozen reubens

"THE SUPPORT OF THE CROWD EVERY TIME I CAME INTO THE RING AND THE ENTHUSIASM WAS JUST A GREAT FEELING."

—MICHAEL MATZ

Devon Turf Club Miniature Burger Bites

1 pound ground beef
Salt and pepper to taste
Oregano to taste
Garlic powder to taste
Basil to taste
1 baguette, cut into 24 slices
1/2 cup sour cream
3 to 4 tablespoons horseradish
Paprika (optional)

Mix the ground beef with salt, pepper, oregano, garlic powder and basil according to taste in a bowl. Shape into patties just big enough to fit the baguette slices. Place one patty on each baguette slice and arrange on a baking sheet.

Broil for 3 to 4 minutes or until cooked through. Mix the sour cream and horseradish in a bowl and top each burger with a dollop of the mixture. Sprinkle with paprika for a dash of color. Serve immediately.

Makes 2 dozen burger bites

TENDERLOIN TEA SANDWICHES

1 peppercorn pork tenderloin or plain pork tenderloin
1 French bread baguette, cut into 1/2-inch slices
1 (3-ounce) jar pesto
4 ounces Asiago cheese, thinly sliced

Roast the tenderloin, covered, at 375 degrees for 40 minutes. Remove the cover and roast for 10 minutes longer. Let stand until cool. Cut into 1/4-inch slices.

Spread one side of each baguette slice with pesto. Layer each pesto side with one slice of cheese and one slice of pork. Chill, covered, for 1 hour and serve. **MAKES 25 to 30 sandwiches**

PARTY DOGS

Party dogs
Mustard of choice

Obtain an accurate head count of your guests. Try to determine if any of your guests have participated in the Nathan's Famous Fourth of July International Hot Dog Eating Contest.

Make sure the Lancaster County Farmers Market in Strafford is open. They are usually open Wednesdays, Fridays and Saturdays and the day before the Christmas holiday but they are not open on most holidays. Travel to the Lancaster County Farmers Market in Strafford and purchase at least three party dogs per person or more depending on your guest list and whether or not any of them are former Nathan's Famous Champions.

Freeze party dogs to be used or snacked on at a later date or cook as directed. Serve hot while soaking up the compliments. Do not forget the mustard. **MAKES a variable amount**

Roasted Chicken Salad Bites

1 (2- to 3-pound) chicken
1/4 cup olive oil
1 teaspoon salt
1/2 teaspoon pepper
3/4 cup mayonnaise
1 cup seedless red grapes, sliced
1 (11-ounce) can mandarin oranges, drained
2 tablespoons chopped fresh dill weed
1/2 cup sunflower seeds
24 miniature croissants, split into halves

Brush the chicken with olive oil and sprinkle with salt and pepper. Wrap in foil and roast at 350 degrees for 1 to 1 1/2 hours or until a meat thermometer inserted in the thickest portion registers 165 degrees. Let cool until easily handled. Chop the chicken, discarding the skin and bones.

Combine the mayonnaise, grapes, oranges, dill weed and sunflower seeds in a bowl and mix well. Stir in the chicken. Spread on the bottom half of each croissant and top with the croissant tops. Arrange on a serving platter and chill, covered, until serving time. **MAKES 2 dozen**

CUCUMBER SANDWICHES

1 loaf melba thin white bread, crusts trimmed
    (Arnold preferred)
1 cucumber, peeled and cut into paper-thin slices
2 tablespoons Jane's Krazy Mixed-Up salt
1 cup mayonnaise-type salad dressing
3 tablespoons dried minced onion flakes
Dash of Worcestershire sauce

Cut the bread slices into quarters and store in a sealable plastic bag. Combine the cucumber and salt with enough water to cover in a bowl. Marinate for several hours or for up to 10 hours. Drain the cucumber and place on paper towels.

Combine the salad dressing, onion flakes and Worcestershire sauce in a bowl and mix well. Spread some of the mixture on each bread quarter and layer with two or three cucumber slices. Arrange the sandwiches on a serving platter and cover with plastic wrap. Chill until serving time. **MAKES 50-plus sandwiches**

STUFFED, WRAPPED AND ROLLED

The ringmaster sounds the horn for the start of evening session of classes at the Devon Horse Show.

LADIES' SIDESADDLE

MINT ZINGER PUNCH

CHAMPAGNE WHITE PEACH SOUP

CRAB CLAWS WITH MUSTARD SAUCE

CUCUMBER SANDWICHES

FRIED MOZZARELLA STICKS

FOIE GRAS STUFFED DATES

6 large Medjool dates, cut lengthwise into halves and pitted
2 ounces foie gras (goose liver)
Fleur de Sel (French sea salt)
Chopped fresh parsley

Stuff each date half with a heaping 1/2 teaspoon of the foie gras. Sprinkle with salt and parsley. Arrange the stuffed dates on a serving platter and chill, covered, until serving time. SERVES 4

THESE ARE PERFECT FOR THANKSGIVING.

BACON AND TOMATO CUPS

8 slices bacon
3 ounces Swiss cheese, shredded
1 tomato, chopped
1/2 onion, chopped
1 teaspoon dried basil
1/2 cup mayonnaise
1 (8-count) can refrigerator buttermilk biscuits

Cook the bacon in a skillet over medium heat until brown and crisp; drain. Crumble the bacon into a medium bowl and stir in the cheese, tomato, onion and basil. Add the mayonnaise and stir until combined.

Separate the biscuits horizontally into halves. Fit each biscuit half into a lightly greased miniature muffin cup. Fill each biscuit-lined cup evenly with the bacon mixture. Bake at 375 degrees for 10 to 12 minutes or until golden brown. MAKES 16 cups

Petite French Onion Phyllo Cups

2 tablespoons unsalted butter
1 tablespoon olive oil
1 large sweet onion, thinly sliced and chopped
   (Vidalia or Walla Walla preferred)
1 teaspoon sugar
1 teaspoon fresh thyme, or
   1/2 teaspoon dried thyme
Salt and pepper to taste
2 (15-count) packages frozen miniature
   phyllo shells
8 ounces Gruyère cheese or Swiss cheese,
   cut into small cubes

Heat the butter and olive oil in a skillet until the butter melts and add the onion. Sauté over high heat for 5 minutes and reduce the heat to low. Sprinkle the sugar, thyme, salt and pepper over the onion. Cook, covered, for 20 to 25 minutes or until the onion is golden brown and caramelized, stirring occasionally and adding water or wine if the mixture becomes too dry.

Layer each phyllo shell with a few cheese cubes, a spoonful of the onion mixture and a few more cheese cubes. Bake at 350 degrees for 20 minutes or until bubbly. **Makes 30 cups**

For a different flavor, mix in 1/2 cup dry white wine or three minced bacon slices or an equal portion of prosciutto with the onion. The addition of the bacon or prosciutto will result in a smoky flavor.

GREEK OLIVE CUPS

1 cup pecan pieces, toasted
1 cup (4 ounces) shredded
   Cheddar cheese
1 cup chopped pimento-
   stuffed olives

2 tablespoons mayonnaise
2 (15-count) packages frozen
   miniature phyllo shells

Combine the pecans, cheese, olives and mayonnaise in a bowl and mix well. Remove the phyllo shells from the freezer, leaving them in the tray. Spoon 1 teaspoon of the olive mixture into each shell. Place the tray in a sealable freezer bag and freeze for up to 1 month.

Arrange the frozen shells on a baking sheet and let stand for 10 minutes. Bake at 375 degrees for 12 minutes. Serve immediately. Or, bake immediately after assembly at the same temperature and for the same amount of time.
MAKES 30 cups

GOAT CHEESE AND PANCETTA TARTLETS

2 tablespoons butter
1/2 onion, thinly sliced
1 tablespoon minced garlic
1 pint (2 cups) heavy cream
8 ounces goat cheese
4 egg yolks, beaten

6 slices pancetta, cooked, drained
   and crumbled
Dash of salt and pepper
2 (15-count) packages frozen
   miniature phyllo shells

Melt the butter in a sauté pan. Add the onion and garlic and sauté until the onion is tender. Stir in the cream and simmer over low heat for 7 minutes. Remove from the heat and immediately stir in the cheese.

Add the yolks gradually, stirring until combined after each addition. Stir in the pancetta, salt and pepper. Spoon the mixture evenly into the phyllo shells and arrange the filled shells on a baking sheet. Bake at 350 degrees for 12 to 15 minutes or until light brown. Or, freeze unbaked for future use.
MAKES 30 tartlets

PECAN BRIE TARTS

1 (11-ounce) package pie crust mix,
*   or 1 unbaked pie pastry*

4 ounces Brie cheese
1/4 cup ground pecans

Prepare the pie crust mix using package directions. Divide the pastry equally into thirty-six portions and roll each portion into a ball. Press each pastry ball over the bottom and up the side of a 2-inch tart pan. Prick the sides and bottoms of the pastry shells with a fork.

Bake at 375 degrees for 8 to 10 minutes or until light brown and crisp, pressing down on the pastry shells midway through the baking process to retain the shape. Maintain the oven temperature.

Cut the cheese into thirty-six 1/2-inch cubes. Place one cube in each pastry shell. Sprinkle equally with the pecans. Bake for 5 minutes or until bubbly. Serve hot. **MAKES 3 dozen tarts**

SHRIMP CURRY

1 cup mayonnaise
1 hard-cooked egg, finely chopped
1 teaspoon finely grated fresh ginger,
*   or 1/2 teaspoon ginger powder*
1 teaspoon minced green onion
*   (white and green parts)*

1 teaspoon curry powder
1/2 teaspoon garlic
2 (4-ounce) cans shrimp, drained
*   and rinsed*
Puff pastry, toast or crackers

Combine the mayonnaise, egg, ginger, green onion, curry powder and garlic in a bowl and mix well. Stir in the shrimp. Chill, covered, for several hours to allow the flavors to blend. Fill puff pastry with the shrimp mixture, or serve on toast rounds or crackers. **SERVES 10 to 12**

CRAB AND ARTICHOKE-STUFFED MUSHROOMS

8 ounces crab meat, drained and flaked
   (lump crab meat preferred)
1 (14-ounce) can artichoke hearts,
   drained and finely chopped
1 cup mayonnaise
1/2 cup (2 ounces) grated Parmesan cheese
1/4 teaspoon lemon pepper
1/8 teaspoon salt
1/8 teaspoon ground red pepper
30 large mushrooms

Combine the crab meat, artichokes, mayonnaise, cheese, lemon pepper, salt and red pepper in a bowl and mix well. Remove the stems from the mushrooms and discard.

Mound the crab meat mixture in the mushroom caps and arrange the caps in a single layer in a lightly greased shallow baking dish. Bake at 400 degrees for 10 minutes or until hot and bubbly. **MAKES 30**

YOU MAY SUBSTITUTE A MIXTURE OF 1/2 CUP MAYONNAISE AND 1/2 CUP PLAIN YOGURT FOR 1 CUP MAYONNAISE, IF DESIRED.

Stuffed High-Crown Mushrooms

1 pound fresh white mushrooms
    (about 25 to 30)
1 pound bulk country sausage
1 garlic clove, minced
1 (8-ounce) can tomato sauce
1 cup white wine
1/4 teaspoon oregano

Remove the stems from the mushrooms and finely chop the stems. Combine the stems with the sausage and garlic in a bowl and mix well. Mound the mixture in the mushroom caps and round to a high crown. Arrange the mushrooms in a single layer in a baking dish and bake at 350 degrees for 30 minutes. Maintain the oven temperature.

Combine the tomato sauce, wine and oregano in a saucepan and cook until heated through. Arrange the mushrooms in a deep baking pan and add the warm wine sauce, adding additional wine if needed to cover the mushrooms. Bake for 10 minutes longer. Remove to a chafing dish to serve. **Serves 8 to 10**

MUSHROOMS IN GARLIC BUTTER

2 dozen large mushrooms
1/2 cup (1 stick) butter, softened
1/2 cup minced parsley
2 garlic cloves, minced
2 shallots, minced
1/2 teaspoon fresh lemon juice
1/2 teaspoon salt
1/4 teaspoon pepper

Remove the stems from the mushrooms and discard the stems. Combine the butter, parsley, garlic and shallots in a food processor or small bowl and process or mix until combined. Add the lemon juice, salt and pepper and process briefly.

Fill the mushroom caps evenly with the garlic butter mixture and arrange in a single layer in a shallow baking dish. Bake at 400 degrees for 10 to 12 minutes or until bubbly. **MAKES 2 dozen**

MUSHROOMS PARMESAN

12 large mushrooms
2 tablespoons butter
1 onion, minced
2 ounces pepperoni, chopped (about 1/2 cup)
1/4 cup chopped green bell pepper
1 small garlic clove, minced
1/3 cup chicken broth
3 tablespoons grated Parmesan cheese
1 tablespoon parsley
1/2 teaspoon seasoned salt
1/4 teaspoon oregano
Dash of pepper

Remove the stems from the mushrooms and chop the stems. Melt the butter in a skillet and add the chopped mushroom stems, onion, pepperoni, bell pepper and garlic. Cook until the onion is tender. Stir in the broth, cheese, parsley, seasoned salt, oregano and pepper and cook just until combined.

Mound the mixture in the mushroom caps and arrange the mushrooms in a single layer in a shallow baking pan. Add enough water to the baking pan to measure 1/4 inch. Bake at 325 degrees for 25 minutes. **MAKES 1 dozen**

BAKED POTATO SKINS

8 (8-ounce) russet potatoes
Olive oil
Sweet paprika to taste
Fine sea salt or kosher salt to taste
Pepper to taste

Rub the potatoes with olive oil and pierce each potato in several places with a fork. Arrange the potatoes on the middle oven rack and bake at 425 degrees for 1 hour. Let stand until cool. Cut the potatoes lengthwise into halves. Scoop out the pulp, leaving a 1/4-inch shell. Reserve the potato pulp for another use. Maintain the oven temperature.

Cut each shell lengthwise into six strips and arrange the strips on a baking sheet. Brush the strips with olive oil and sprinkle with paprika, salt and pepper. Bake on the middle oven rack for 20 to 25 minutes or until golden brown and crisp. Serve with sour cream. SERVES 6

LOBSTER DEVILED EGGS

2 dozen eggs
Salt to taste
1 (1¹/₄-pound) lobster, steamed,
  shelled and chopped
1 tablespoon mustard
3 shallots, minced
2 tablespoons mayonnaise
2 tablespoons capers
1 bunch chives, trimmed and minced
Pepper to taste

Simmer the eggs in lightly salted water in a saucepan for 12 to 15 minutes. Run the eggs under cold water until cool. Cut the eggs horizontally into halves and remove the yolks. Save the yolks for another use.

Combine the lobster, mustard, shallots, mayonnaise, capers and chives in a bowl and mix well. Season with salt and pepper. Fill the egg whites evenly with the lobster mixture. Arrange on a serving platter and garnish with additional chives. MAKES **4 dozen halves**

DEVILED EGGS

1 dozen hard-cooked eggs
3/4 cup mayonnaise
2 teaspoons Champagne mustard (Cherchies preferred)
2 teaspoons aged sherry vinegar
2 teaspoons chopped fresh parsley
2 teaspoons chopped fresh thyme
Salt and pepper to taste
2 teaspoons chopped fresh chives or salmon caviar

Cut the eggs lengthwise into halves. Remove the yolks to a food processor and process until finely chopped. Add the mayonnaise, Champagne mustard and vinegar and process until blended. Stir in the parsley and thyme and season with salt and pepper.

Pipe the mixture into the egg whites and arrange the eggs on a serving platter. Sprinkle with the chives. Chill, covered, until serving time. **MAKES 2 dozen halves**

Devilish Eggs

1 dozen hard-cooked eggs, peeled
6 tablespoons mayonnaise
1/4 cup horseradish
2 tablespoons sweet pickle juice
1 teaspoon freshly ground pepper
1/4 teaspoon salt

Cut the eggs lengthwise into halves and remove the yolks to a bowl. Mash the yolks. Combine with the mayonnaise, horseradish, pickle juice, pepper and salt in a food processor and process until smooth. Mound the mixture in the egg whites and arrange on a serving platter. Chill, covered, until serving time.
Makes 2 dozen halves

Chutney-Stuffed Eggs

1 dozen hard-cooked eggs
1/4 cup chutney
6 slices bacon, crisp-cooked and crumbled
3 tablespoons mayonnaise
2 tablespoons chopped fresh parsley

Cut the eggs lengthwise into halves and remove the yolks to a bowl. Mash the yolks. Add the chutney, bacon and mayonnaise and stir until combined. Mound the mixture in the egg whites and arrange on a serving platter. Sprinkle with the parsley. Chill, covered, until serving time. **Makes 2 dozen halves**

Miniature Beef Wellingtons with Madeira Sauce

BEEF WELLINGTONS

1 (17-ounce) package frozen
    puff pastry
1/3 cup boursin cheese, softened
    (about 2 1/2 ounces)
8 ounces filet mignon, trimmed and
    cut into 1/2-inch cubes
Salt and freshly ground pepper
    to taste
1 egg, lightly beaten

MADEIRA SAUCE

2 tablespoons butter
1/2 cup chopped onion
1/4 cup minced celery
1/4 cup minced carrot
2 tablespoons all-purpose flour
2 cups canned beef broth
1/2 cup chopped seeded tomato
1/2 cup Madeira
1/2 teaspoon chopped fresh thyme

To prepare the Wellingtons, roll each pastry sheet into a 1/8-inch-thick 7×15-inch rectangle on a lightly floured sheet of baking parchment. Cut the pastry into 1 1/2-inch squares. Spoon about 1/4 teaspoon of the cheese in the center of each square.

Season the beef with salt and pepper and arrange one cube of beef on each pastry square. Fold the pastry over the beef, tucking in the corners to seal. Arrange the pastries seam side down on a large baking sheet lined with baking parchment. May prepare to this point and freeze for up to 1 week. Lightly brush each pastry with the egg. Bake at 400 degrees for 10 to 12 minutes or until puffed and golden brown. Let cool slightly and arrange on a serving platter.

To prepare the sauce, melt the butter in a heavy saucepan over medium heat. Add the onion, celery and carrot and sauté for 25 minutes or just until the vegetables begin to brown. Add the flour and cook for 8 minutes or until the flour browns, stirring constantly. Add the broth gradually and bring to a boil, whisking constantly. Reduce the heat to low and stir in the tomato.

Simmer for 10 minutes or until the sauce begins to thicken, stirring frequently. Remove from the heat and let cool slightly. Process the sauce in batches in a blender until puréed. Return the purée to the saucepan and stir in the wine and thyme. Bring to a boil and reduce the heat. Simmer for 5 minutes or until of a sauce consistency, whisking occasionally. Serve with the Beef Wellingtons. The sauce may be prepared up to 1 day in advance and stored, covered, in the refrigerator. Reheat before serving. MAKES 4 dozen miniature Wellingtons

GRAND PRIX PROSCIUTTO

1 (20-ounce) jar roasted red peppers, drained
8 ounces prosciutto, thinly sliced and
  cut horizontally into halves
  (Boar's Head preferred)
1 large container fresh honeydew melon

Slice the roasted peppers into $1/2 \times 3$-inch strips. Wrap each pepper strip with one piece of prosciutto. Chill in a sealable plastic bag for 8 to 10 hours to enhance the flavor.

Slice the honeydew melon approximately the same size as the roasted peppers on the day of service. Wrap one piece of melon with one piece of prosciutto and secure with a decorative wooden pick. Store in a sealable plastic bag in the refrigerator until serving time. Each variation makes approximately twenty-five.
MAKES 50

THIS IS A QUICK AND EASY APPETIZER THAT TRAVELS WELL AND IS NOT ADVERSELY AFFECTED BY WARM WEATHER.

Fresh Figs in a Blanket

1/2 cup crumbled Gorgonzola cheese
6 small to medium fresh ripe figs, stems removed and
*   cut into quarters*
2 tablespoons balsamic vinegar
2 tablespoons walnut oil or olive oil
8 ounces prosciutto, cut into 1 1/2 × 5 1/2-inch strips

Place about 1/2 teaspoon of the cheese on each fig quarter, pressing gently into the bottom portion of the fig. Whisk the vinegar and walnut oil in a bowl and brush each fig with the mixture. Wrap each with a strip of prosciutto. Arrange on a serving platter and serve immediately, or chill, covered, until serving time. **MAKES 2 dozen**

Prosciutto Wraps

6 ripe pears, sliced
Fresh lemon juice
2 (5-ounce) packages herb cheese, softened
*   (such as boursin)*
60 arugula leaves
1/3 pound prosciutto, thinly sliced and
*   cut into long strips*

Toss the sliced pears with lemon juice in a bowl to prevent browning. Stack one pear slice, a small dollop of cheese and one arugula leaf on the end of each strip of prosciutto. Wrap the prosciutto around the stacks until secure. **MAKES 5 dozen wraps**

BACON-WRAPPED SHRIMP WITH SPICY ORANGE SAUCE

SPICY ORANGE SAUCE

6 tablespoons orange marmalade
2 hot red chiles, stemmed and chopped, or
   1/2 teaspoon red pepper flakes
4 green onions, chopped (white and green parts)
1/4 cup chopped fresh cilantro
1/4 cup extra-virgin olive oil
Salt and pepper to taste

SHRIMP

16 large shrimp, peeled and deveined
6 to 8 slices bacon, cut onto 2- to 3-inch pieces

To prepare the sauce, combine the marmalade, red chiles, green onions, cilantro, olive oil, salt and pepper in a bowl and mix well.

To prepare the shrimp, wrap each shrimp with one piece of bacon and secure with a wooden pick. Arrange in a single layer on a baking sheet.

Broil for 2 to 3 minutes or until the shrimp turn pink and the bacon is crisp, turning once. Remove the shrimp to a platter and serve immediately with the sauce. SERVES 4 to 6

MPI Shrimp

DIPPING SAUCE
1 bottle French salad dressing
$^1/_2$ (5-ounce) jar good-quality strong horseradish
Juice of $^1/_2$ lemon

SHRIMP
1 pound jumbo shrimp, peeled and deveined
1 (5-ounce) jar good-quality horseradish
Bacon, cut into halves

To prepare the sauce, combine the salad dressing, horseradish and lemon juice in a bowl and mix well. Chill, covered, until serving time.

To prepare the shrimp, cut a slit in each shrimp to make a pocket. Stuff the pockets with horseradish and wrap each shrimp with one bacon half. Secure with wooden picks. Arrange the shrimp on a baking sheet and broil until the bacon is crisp on both sides and the shrimp turn pink, turning once. SERVES **10 to 12**

THESE ARE A LONGTIME FAVORITE OF THE MILE POST INN.

CRABBY JACK QUESADILLAS

2 cups (8 ounces) shredded Monterey Jack cheese
1 cup thinly sliced green onions
    (white and green parts)
4 ounces crab meat, drained and flaked
10 flour tortillas

Combine the cheese, green onions and crab meat in a bowl and mix well. Arrange five of the tortillas in a single layer on a baking sheet. Spread the crab meat mixture evenly on the tortillas and top with the remaining tortillas.

Bake at 450 degrees for 7 minutes. Cut each quesadilla into six wedges. Serve warm with salsa. **MAKES 30 wedges**

GOAT CHEESE QUESADILLA

Vegetable oil
2 (8-inch) flour tortillas
4 slices provolone cheese
2 tablespoons chopped red bell peppers
1 tablespoon chopped fresh rosemary
1/4 cup crumbled goat cheese

Lightly coat a skillet with oil. Place one of the tortillas in the prepared skillet and layer with the provolone cheese, bell peppers, rosemary and goat cheese. Top with the remaining tortilla.

Cook until the cheese melts and the bottom is light brown. Turn the quesadilla and continue cooking until the remaining side is light brown. Cut into wedges with kitchen shears and garnish with a sprig of rosemary. **MAKES 4 to 6 wedges**

PEACH AND BRIE QUESADILLAS

LIME HONEY DIPPING SAUCE
2 tablespoons honey
2 teaspoons fresh lime juice
1/2 teaspoon grated lime zest

QUESADILLA
1 cup thinly sliced peeled peaches
*   (about 2 large)*
1 tablespoon chopped fresh chives
1 teaspoon brown sugar
4 (8-inch) flour tortillas
3 ounces Brie cheese, thinly sliced

To prepare the sauce, whisk the honey, lime juice and lime zest in a bowl until combined.

To prepare the quesadilla, gently toss the peaches with the chives and brown sugar in a bowl until coated. Top each tortilla with one-fourth of the cheese and one-fourth of the peach mixture and fold over to enclose the filling.

Heat a large nonstick skillet over medium-high heat until hot and spray with nonstick cooking spray. Place two quesadillas in the prepared pan and cook for 2 minutes on each side or until the quesadillas are light brown and crisp. Remove to a baking sheet and cover to keep warm. Repeat the procedure with the remaining quesadillas. Cut each quesadilla into three wedges and garnish with strips of fresh chives. Serve warm with the sauce. **MAKES 12 wedges**

RIPE BUT FIRM PEACHES WORK BEST. IF THE PEACHES ARE TOO RIPE, THE QUESADILLAS WILL BE SOGGY. PLACING THE FILLINGS ON ONE SIDE OF THE TORTILLA AND FOLDING THE OTHER HALF OVER LIKE A TACO MAKES THE QUESADILLAS EASIER TO HANDLE.

MINIATURE SPANAKOPITA

1/2 cup ricotta cheese
2 tablespoons butter
1/4 cup finely minced onion
1 (10-ounce) package frozen creamed spinach
1 tablespoon pepper
1 teaspoon ground nutmeg
3 ounces reduced-fat feta cheese, crumbled
1 (16-ounce) package phyllo pastry,
*   thawed in the refrigerator*
Extra-virgin olive oil

Drain the ricotta cheese through several layers of cheesecloth in a colander, pressing out all the moisture. Melt the butter in a sauté pan over medium heat. Add the onion and sauté until tender and slightly caramelized. Stir in the spinach, pepper and nutmeg.

Cook for 5 minutes, stirring occasionally. Remove from the heat and stir in the ricotta cheese and feta cheese. Let stand until cool and chill, covered, for 20 minutes or longer.

Cut the phyllo pastry starting from the long side into 2-inch-wide strips. Cover with waxed paper and a damp kitchen towel to keep moist. Remove three strips at a time and stack. Brush the top strip lightly with olive oil. Place 2 teaspoons of the spinach mixture 1/2 inch above the bottom corner. Fold into a triangle shape and repeat as though folding a flag. Repeat the procedure with the remaining phyllo strips, olive oil and the remaining spinach mixture.

Arrange the triangles seam side down on a baking sheet lined with baking parchment. Lightly brush the triangles with olive oil and bake at 375 degrees for 20 minutes or until golden brown. Serve warm. **MAKES 5 dozen**

STROMBOLI

Frozen pizza dough, at room temperature
12 to 16 ounces assorted deli Italian meats
(prosciutto, mortadella, capocola,
Genoa salami, Italian ham)
1/2 cup (2 ounces) grated Parmesan cheese
1/2 cup (2 ounces) shredded sharp provolone cheese
1 egg yolk, lightly beaten
Poppy seeds or sesame seeds (optional)

Divide the dough into two equal portions. Roll each portion into an
8×10-inch rectangle on a lightly floured surface. Layer the deli meats, Parmesan
cheese and provolone cheese to within 1 inch of the edges on both rectangles.

Roll as for a jelly roll and pinch the ends to seal. Arrange the stromboli seam
side down on a baking sheet. Cut diagonal slashes in the top of each stromboli
every 2 inches to allow the steam to exit. Brush with the egg yolk and sprinkle
with poppy seeds. Bake at 375 degrees for 45 minutes. Slice as desired. Serve hot
or chilled. **SERVES 6 to 8**

BACON-WRAPPED WATER CHESTNUTS

2 (8-ounce) cans whole water chestnuts, drained
Soy sauce
Brown sugar
1 pound sliced bacon, cut into halves

Soak the water chestnuts in enough soy sauce to cover in a bowl for 2 hours; drain. Roll the water chestnuts in brown sugar.

Wrap each water chestnut with one-half slice of bacon and secure with a wooden pick. Arrange on a rack in a baking pan. Bake at 350 degrees for 45 minutes. Serve hot. **SERVES 10 to 12**

"THE DEVON HORSE SHOW AND COUNTRY FAIR IS ABOUT VOLUNTEERS AND TRADITION. WE HAVE TWO ITEMS AS PART OF THE DEVON TRADITION THAT FALL INTO THE CATEGORY OF FOOD—DEVON FUDGE AND DEVON LEMON STICKS—MADE BY VOLUNTEERS AND AVAILABLE SINCE THE EARLY YEARS OF THE HORSE SHOW."

—LEONARD KING
CEO, DEVON HORSE SHOW FOUNDATION

Rumaki

1/3 cup soy sauce
2 tablespoons dry sherry
1 garlic clove, minced
1/8 teaspoon pepper
8 ounces chicken livers
1 (8-ounce) can whole water chestnuts, drained
8 ounces sliced bacon, cut into halves

Mix the soy sauce, sherry, garlic and pepper in a bowl. Add the chicken livers and stir until coated. Marinate in the refrigerator for 30 minutes, stirring occasionally; drain.

Cut the water chestnuts into thirds. Wrap one chicken liver and one water chestnut third with one-half slice of bacon and secure with a wooden pick. Arrange on a rack in a baking pan. Bake at 400 degrees for 20 minutes or until the bacon is brown and crisp. **SERVES 6 to 8**

Beoreg (Bed-Egg) Armenian Appetizer

16 ounces Muenster cheese, shredded
8 ounces pot-style cottage cheese (large curd)
2 eggs, lightly beaten
¹/₂ teaspoon salt
Chopped parsley
1 (16-ounce) package phyllo pastry
Melted butter

Combine the Muenster cheese, cottage cheese, eggs, salt and parsley in a bowl and mix well. Cover the pastry sheets with waxed paper and a damp kitchen towel to keep moist. Cut each sheet into 4-inch-wide strips.

Place 1 tablespoon of the cheese filling at the end of each strip. Fold into a triangle shape and repeat as though folding a flag. Arrange the triangles on a baking sheet lined with parchment paper. Brush with melted butter and bake at 400 degrees until light brown. Serve hot. **MAKES 32 to 40**

ONCE BAKED, THESE MAY BE PLACED BETWEEN SHEETS OF WAXED PAPER AND FROZEN. THAW COMPLETELY BEFORE WARMING IN THE OVEN.

BRIE IN PUFF PASTRY

1 sheet frozen puff pastry, thawed in the refrigerator
1 (16-ounce) round Brie cheese
¹/₂ cup apricot preserves
1 egg
1 teaspoon water

Roll the pastry on a lightly floured surface into a round large enough to enclose the cheese. Place the cheese in the center of the pastry round and spread with the preserves. Brush the edges of the pastry with a mixture of the egg and water and bring up the pastry to enclose the cheese, overlapping and pleating as needed. Cut off the excess pastry and be creative arranging the scraps atop the pastry. Place the pastry on a baking sheet.

Brush the top with the egg wash and bake at 400 degrees for 20 minutes. Serve with sliced apples and/or assorted crackers. SERVES 12

Spiral Reuben Dijon Bites

1 sheet frozen puff pastry, thawed in the refrigerator
1/4 cup Dijon mustard
3/4 cup (3 ounces) shredded Swiss cheese
6 to 8 slices deli corned beef (about 6 ounces)
1 egg, beaten
1 tablespoon caraway seeds

Roll the pastry into a 10×12-inch rectangle on a lightly floured surface. Spread the pastry with the Dijon mustard and layer with the cheese and corned beef. Cut the rectangle crosswise into halves. Roll each rectangle as for a jelly roll and seal the ends. You may wrap and freeze for future use at this point. Thaw at room temperature for 30 minutes before proceeding with the recipe.

Cut each roll into sixteen slices. Arrange each slice cut side up on a lightly greased baking sheet. Brush with the egg and sprinkle with the caraway seeds. Bake at 400 degrees for 10 to 12 minutes or until golden brown. Serve warm with additional Dijon mustard. **MAKES 32 bites**

PROSCIUTTO AND GRUYÈRE PINWHEELS

³/4 cup (3 ounces) finely grated Gruyère cheese
1 tablespoon chopped fresh sage
1 sheet frozen puff pastry, thawed in the refrigerator
1 egg, lightly beaten
2 ounces prosciutto, thinly sliced

Mix the cheese and sage in a bowl. Place the pastry sheet on a lightly floured surface with the short side facing you and cut crosswise into halves. Arrange one pastry half with the long side facing you and brush the edge of the far side with some of the egg. Arrange half the prosciutto evenly on the pastry, avoiding the egg-brushed edge, and top with half the cheese mixture. Starting with the side nearest you, roll as for a jelly roll and wrap in waxed paper. Place the log on a baking sheet seam side down. Repeat the process with the remaining pastry half, remaining egg, remaining prosciutto and remaining cheese mixture.

Chill for 3 hours up to 3 days or until firm. Cut the logs crosswise into ¹/2-inch pinwheels and arrange cut sides down 1 inch apart on two lightly greased baking sheets. Bake at 400 degrees for 14 to 16 minutes or until golden brown. Remove to a wire rack to cool slightly. **MAKES about 40 pinwheels**

Pizza Wheels

16 ounces mozzarella cheese
1 (8-ounce) pepperoni stick, chopped
3 eggs, lightly beaten
2 tablespoons dried oregano
1 (8-count) can refrigerator crescent rolls

Process the cheese in a food processor until finely chopped. Process the pepperoni in a food processor until finely chopped. Combine the cheese, pepperoni, eggs and oregano in a bowl and mix well.

Separate the crescent roll dough into four rectangles, sealing the perforations. Roll the rectangles into $6^1/2 \times 8^1/2$-inch rectangles on a lightly floured surface. Divide the pepperoni mixture into four equal portions and spread one portion on each rectangle.

Roll the rectangles as for a jelly roll, starting at the short end. Moisten the seams with a little water to seal. Arrange the rolls on a greased baking sheet and freeze for 45 minutes or until firm but not frozen.

Cut the rolls into $1/4$- to $1/2$-inch slices. Bake at 350 degrees for 10 to 12 minutes or until golden brown. Remove to a wire rack. You may freeze the unbaked slices in sealable freezer bags for future use. Extend the baking time slightly for frozen slices. **MAKES about 3 dozen**

SAUSAGE ROLLS

2¹/₂ pounds sage sausage
1 large white onion, finely chopped
8 ounces sliced bacon
2 to 3 tablespoons chopped mixed fresh herbs
*   such as parsley, marjoram, thyme or tarragon*
1 (17-ounce) package frozen puff pastry,
*   thawed in the refrigerator*
6 hard-cooked eggs, sliced
Salt and pepper to taste
1 egg
1 teaspoon water

Brown the sausage with the onion in a skillet, stirring until the sausage is crumbly; drain. Mash the mixture until all lumps have disappeared. Cook the bacon in a skillet until brown and crisp; drain. Crumble the bacon. Combine with the sausage mixture and herbs in a bowl and mix well.

Roll the pastry sheets into 7×15-inch rectangles. Divide the sausage mixture evenly between the two pastry sheets. Arrange the egg slices over the centers of the sausage mixture. Season with salt and pepper. Fold the short ends of the pastry sheets up and roll to enclose the filling. Place on a baking sheet.

Whisk the egg and water together in a small bowl. Brush the sausage rolls with the egg wash. Bake at 375 degrees for 30 minutes. Let cool to room temperature and slice into individual servings. **SERVES 6 to 10**

TURKEY APPETIZER WRAPS

2 (5-ounce) packages boursin cheese, softened
10 (any flavor) flour tortillas
8 ounces roasted red peppers, cut into 1-inch slices
1 bunch fresh basil, trimmed and stems removed
2 pounds sliced luncheon turkey breast
3 tablespoons mayonnaise

Spread the cheese on one side of each tortilla. Arrange a row of roasted peppers and a row of basil down the center of each tortilla and cover with a single layer of turkey. Top with a dollop of mayonnaise.

Roll the tortillas tightly to enclose the filling and wrap in plastic wrap. Chill for 1 hour or longer. Slice as desired and serve immediately.

SERVES 10 to 12

ASPARAGUS ROLL-UPS

3 ounces (or more) blue cheese, crumbled
8 ounces cream cheese, softened
1 egg, lightly beaten
1 loaf soft thin-sliced white bread, crusts trimmed
1 (15-ounce) can asparagus spears, drained
2 cups (4 sticks) butter, melted

Mix the blue cheese, cream cheese and egg in a bowl. Roll each slice of bread with a rolling pin until flat. Cover to prevent the bread from drying out.

Remove the bread slices one at a time and spread with some of the cheese mixture. Place one asparagus spear on each slice and roll to enclose. Roll in the butter and arrange seam side down on a baking sheet.

Freeze, covered with waxed paper, for 30 minutes. At this point you may freeze the rolls in sealable plastic freezer bags for future use. Bake at 350 degrees for 20 minutes or until light brown. **MAKES 15 to 20 roll-ups**

MUSHROOM ROLL-UPS

1 large onion, finely chopped
1 teaspoon butter
12 ounces fresh mushrooms, finely chopped
1/4 teaspoon salt
1/8 teaspoon pepper
12 ounces cream cheese, softened and cubed
1/2 teaspoon Worcestershire sauce
1/4 teaspoon garlic powder
1 loaf thin-sliced white bread, crusts trimmed
1/2 to 1 cup (1 to 2 sticks) butter, melted

Sauté the onion in 1 teaspoon butter in a skillet until translucent. Add the mushrooms and sauté for 2 minutes longer. Remove from the heat and stir in the salt and pepper. Add the cream cheese and stir until combined. Mix in the Worcestershire sauce and garlic powder. Let stand until almost cool.

Roll each slice of bread with a rolling pin until flat. Spread a thick layer of the mushroom mixture on each slice of bread and roll as for a jelly roll to enclose the filling. Secure with wooden picks and chill, covered, for 1 hour or until set.

Cut the rolls into 1/4-inch slices and arrange cut side up in a single layer on a baking sheet. Brush with the melted butter. You may freeze at this point in sealable plastic freezer bags for future use. Broil until light brown. Serve immediately. Double the recipe for a large crowd. **Serves 12**

SPREADS

There are 476 stalls inside the grounds and 384 stalls across Valley Forge Road in what we call the New Barns. Thanks to the proper renovations, "the look" will always be Devon.

Scurry Class

Bloody Mary

Red Pepper Soup

MPI Shrimp

Gorgonzola and
Fig Terrine

Petite French Onion
Phyllo Cups

AVALON CRAB MOLD

1 (10-ounce) can tomato soup
1 envelope unflavored gelatin
8 ounces cream cheese, softened
1 cup mayonnaise
1/2 cup chopped celery
1/2 cup chopped onion
8 ounces crab meat, drained and flaked

Bring the soup to a boil in a small saucepan; do not add water. Soften the gelatin in a small amount of water in a bowl and stir into the soup.

Cook until blended, stirring frequently. Remove from the heat and blend in the cream cheese and mayonnaise. Add the celery, onion and crab meat and mix well. Pour into your favorite mold and chill, covered, until firm. Invert onto a serving platter and serve with assorted party crackers or assorted toasted bagel chips. **SERVES 8 to 10**

CRAB MOUSSE MOLD

2 envelopes unflavored gelatin
1/4 cup cold water
6 ounces cream cheese, cubed
1 (10-ounce) can cream of mushroom soup
1 cup mayonnaise
1 teaspoon Worcestershire sauce
1 (6-ounce) can crab meat, drained and flaked
1 cup chopped celery
1 small onion, grated

Soften the gelatin in the cold water in a small bowl and mix well. Mix the cream cheese, soup, mayonnaise and Worcestershire sauce in a saucepan. Cook over low heat until blended, stirring frequently. Stir in the gelatin mixture, crab meat, celery and onion.

Pour into your favorite mold. Chill, covered, until firm. Invert onto a serving platter and serve with assorted party crackers. **SERVES 6 to 8**

Hot Clam Pie

4 (7-ounce) cans clams
4 teaspoons lemon juice
2 small onions, chopped
2 green bell peppers, chopped
1/2 cup parsley, chopped
1 cup (2 sticks) butter, chopped
2 tablespoons oregano
Dash of Tabasco sauce
1/2 teaspoon seasoned pepper
1 1/2 cups bread crumbs
1 cup (4 ounces) shredded mozzarella cheese
1/2 cup (2 ounces) grated Parmesan cheese
Paprika to taste

Drain the clams, reserving the juice. Combine the clams with the lemon juice in a saucepan and bring to a simmer. Simmer for 15 minutes. Mix the onions, bell peppers and parsley with the reserved clam juice in a bowl. Add to the clam mixture and stir in the butter and oregano.

Simmer until the butter melts and then stir in the Tabasco sauce, pepper and bread crumbs. Spoon into a pie plate and sprinkle with the mozzarella cheese, Parmesan cheese and paprika. Bake at 325 degrees until bubbly. Serve warm with Triscuits. You may freeze the unbaked clam pie for future use. Thaw in the refrigerator before baking. **SERVES 6 to 8**

SMOKED OYSTER ROLL

16 ounces cream cheese, cubed and softened
1 garlic clove, crushed
1 tablespoon finely chopped onion
1 tablespoon mayonnaise
1 tablespoon milk
2 teaspoons Worcestershire sauce
1/4 teaspoon salt
1/8 teaspoon white pepper
Dash of Tabasco sauce
2 (3-ounce) cans smoked oysters, drained
1/2 cup finely chopped pistachios, pecans or walnuts

Combine the cream cheese, garlic, onion, mayonnaise, milk, Worcestershire sauce, salt, white pepper and Tabasco sauce in a food processor fitted with a metal blade and process until combined. Shape the mixture into an 8×10-inch rectangle on a baking sheet lined with foil.

Process the oysters in the same bowl until puréed, or mash if desired. Spread over the top of the cream cheese mixture. Chill, loosely covered with plastic wrap, for several hours or until firm. You may chill overnight.

Using a long narrow spatula to help release the cream cheese from the foil, roll as for a jelly roll; do not be concerned if the roll breaks or cracks. Shape into a long roll and completely coat with the pistachios. Chill, wrapped in plastic wrap, for 3 days. Garnish with sprigs of parsley and pimento strips. Serve with assorted party crackers. SERVES **8 to 10**

SHRIMP BUTTER

8 ounces cream cheese, softened
1/4 cup (1/2 stick) butter, softened
2 tablespoons finely minced scallion bulbs
1/4 cup lemon juice
1/4 teaspoon dried dill weed
2 to 4 drops of Tabasco sauce
1/4 teaspoon salt
8 ounces peeled cooked fresh shrimp, coarsely chopped
1 French bread baguette, thinly sliced

Combine the cream cheese, butter, scallions, lemon juice, dill weed, Tabasco sauce and salt in a bowl and mix well. Stir in the shrimp. Spoon into a crock and chill, covered, for 24 hours. Serve with the baguette slices. **SERVES 10 to 12**

SHRIMP LOG

8 ounces Cheddar cheese, shredded
8 ounces cream cheese, softened
1 small onion, grated
1 pound shrimp, cooked, peeled and chopped
1/2 (8-ounce) jar seedless raspberry jam
2 tablespoons white vinegar
1 tablespoon horseradish

Mix the Cheddar cheese, cream cheese and onion in a bowl until combined. Stir in the shrimp. Pat the mixture over the bottom of a serving dish. Mix the jam, vinegar and horseradish in a bowl and spread over the top. Chill, covered, until serving time. Serve with sliced French bread, pita chips and/or fresh vegetables. **SERVES 8 to 10**

SHRIMP MOLD

2 envelopes unflavored gelatin
1/2 cup cold water
1 (10-ounce) can tomato soup
8 ounces cream cheese, cubed and softened
2 (4-ounce) cans small shrimp, chopped
1 cup mayonnaise
3/4 cup minced onion
3/4 cup minced celery
Salt and pepper to taste

Soften the gelatin in the cold water in a small bowl and mix well. Bring the soup to a boil in a saucepan and remove from the heat. Add the cream cheese to the soup and stir until blended. Stir in the gelatin mixture. Let stand until room temperature.

Gradually add the shrimp, mayonnaise, onion, celery, salt and pepper to the soup mixture, mixing well after each addition. Spoon into a greased mold and chill, covered, for 2 to 10 hours or until firm. Invert onto a serving platter and serve with assorted party crackers. **SERVES 6 to 8**

SEAFOOD "PIZZA"

1 cup cocktail sauce
2 teaspoons Old Bay seasoning
16 ounces cream cheese, softened
2 1/2 cups canned baby shrimp
1/4 cup chopped green onions
1/2 cup chopped green bell pepper
1/2 cup sliced black olives
1/2 cup chopped fresh tomato, drained
1/2 cup (2 ounces) grated Parmesan cheese

Mix the cocktail sauce and Old Bay seasoning in a small bowl. Pat the cream cheese over the bottom of a pizza pan or 15-inch round glass tray. Spread with the cocktail sauce mixture.

Sprinkle the shrimp, green onions, bell pepper, olives, tomato and Parmesan cheese in the order listed over the prepared layers. Chill, covered, until serving time. Serve with chips and/or assorted party crackers. SERVES **8 to 10**

SUBSTITUTE CRAB MEAT FOR THE SHRIMP, OR USE A COMBINATION OF THE TWO.

SMOKED BLUEFISH PÂTÉ

1 pound smoked bluefish, skinned and flaked
12 ounces cream cheese, cubed and softened
6 tablespoons unsalted butter, chopped and softened
1 red onion, minced
1/4 cup chopped fresh dill weed
3 tablespoons fresh lemon juice
2 tablespoons Cognac
2 teaspoons capers, drained
Pepper to taste

Mix the fish, cream cheese and butter in a bowl until the ingredients are combined but the fish is still flaky. Add the onion, dill weed, lemon juice, brandy and capers and stir with a wooden spoon until combined. Season with pepper.

Spoon the pâté in a crock or onto a serving platter and chill, covered, for 2 to 10 hours to allow the flavors to blend. Serve at room temperature with toasted French baguette rounds and/or fresh vegetables. SERVES **8 to 10**

SMOKED MACKEREL MAY BE SUBSTITUTED IF SMOKED BLUEFISH IS NOT AVAILABLE FROM YOUR LOCAL FISHMONGER OR SPECIALTY FOOD MARKET. FOR ENHANCED FLAVOR, PREPARE THE PÂTÉ ONE DAY IN ADVANCE.

SMOKED SALMON CHEESE SPREAD

16 ounces cream cheese, softened
1 tablespoon sour cream
1 tablespoon lemon juice, or to taste
1 tablespoon mayonnaise
Dash of Tabasco sauce
Dash of Worcestershire sauce
1/2 cup capers, drained
1/4 cup finely chopped celery
2 green onions or scallions, finely chopped
Dried dill weed
3 cups smoked salmon, chopped into small pieces

Combine the cream cheese, sour cream, lemon juice, mayonnaise, Tabasco sauce and Worcestershire sauce in a bowl and mix until blended. Stir in the capers, celery, green onions and a generous amount of dill weed. Add the salmon and stir just until combined.

Shape the mixture into a ball or spoon into a serving bowl. Chill, covered, until serving time. Serve with assorted party crackers. **SERVES 6 to 8**

SUBSTITUTE CHOPPED COOKED LOBSTER OR CHOPPED COOKED SHRIMP FOR THE SMOKED SALMON, IF DESIRED. IT IS EQUALLY DELICIOUS.

SALMON TERRINE

1 (8-ounce) wild salmon fillet, poached,
*   drained and cooled*
8 ounces smoked salmon
1/2 cup (1 stick) unsalted butter, softened
1/2 cup minced shallots
1/2 cup chopped fresh parsley
2 teaspoons lemon juice
2 teaspoons grated lemon zest
2 teaspoons Champagne mustard
*   (Cherchies preferred)*
2 teaspoons drained capers
2 teaspoons Cognac
Dash of salt and pepper

Process the salmon fillet and smoked salmon in a food processor until chopped. Combine with the butter in a bowl and mix well. Stir in the shallots, parsley, lemon juice, lemon zest, Champagne mustard, capers, brandy, salt and pepper.

Pack the salmon mixture into a terrine. Chill, covered, for 4 to 24 hours. Serve at room temperature with assorted party crackers. SERVES **8 to 10**

HOT SALMON SPREAD

8 ounces cream cheese, softened
1 tablespoon milk
1 (7-ounce) can red salmon,
 drained and flaked
2 tablespoons finely chopped onion

3/4 teaspoon horseradish
1/4 teaspoon salt
1/4 teaspoon freshly ground pepper
1/3 cup slivered almonds

Mix the cream cheese and milk in a bowl until blended. Stir in the salmon, onion, horseradish, salt and pepper. Spread in a baking dish. Reserve some of the almonds for garnish and sprinkle the remaining almonds over the prepared layer.

Bake at 375 degrees for 10 minutes or until heated through. Stir and sprinkle with the reserved almonds. Serve warm with assorted party crackers. **SERVES 6 to 8**

TAKU SMOKERIES FAMOUS PÂTÉ

1 pound smoked hot dried salmon
16 ounces cream cheese, softened
1 cup mayonnaise
1 1/2 teaspoons Dijon mustard

1 1/2 teaspoons lemon juice
1 teaspoon dill weed
Tabasco sauce to taste

Combine the salmon, cream cheese, mayonnaise, Dijon mustard, lemon juice, dill weed and Tabasco sauce in a food processor. Process until well mixed. Spoon the mixture into a crock or serving bowl. Serve with assorted party crackers and/or bagels. **MAKES 2 1/2 pounds**

Sardines and Avocado on Rye

1 ripe avocado, chopped
1 (3-ounce) can sardines, bones removed
Salt and pepper to taste
1 loaf party rye bread

Mash the avocado and sardines in a bowl. Season with salt and pepper. Spread on slices of party rye and arrange on a serving platter. SERVES **8 to 10**

"As show manager, when I asked the director in charge of the ill-fated ostrich exhibition, after he was informed that there would be no more performances during the Devon Horse Show, where he was headed, he replied, 'to join up with my brother at a small county fair in northeast Pennsylvania.' When asked about his brother, he replied, 'Dennis Rivers had Diving Mules!!!!!!'"

—Peter Doubleday
    Show Manager, Devon Horse Show

SMOKED TROUT MOUSSE

8 ounces smoked trout, skinned, boned and flaked
1/2 cup sour cream
1 small shallot, minced
2 tablespoons shredded fresh horseradish
1/4 teaspoon white pepper
1/8 teaspoon salt
1/8 teaspoon ground red pepper
1/4 cup chopped fresh dill weed

Combine the trout, sour cream, shallot, horseradish, white pepper, salt and red pepper in a bowl or food processor and mix or process until combined. Chill, covered, in the refrigerator. Stir in the dill weed just before serving. Serve with toast rounds and/or assorted party crackers. **SERVES 6 to 8**

SMOKED TROUT AND SHRIMP PÂTÉ

12 ounces smoked trout, skinned, boned and
*   torn into small pieces*
12 ounces cooked bay shrimp, peeled
12 ounces cream cheese, softened
3/4 cup chopped fresh chives or green onion tops
3 tablespoons drained capers
1 tablespoon grated lemon zest
Salt and pepper to taste
1 loaf cocktail pumpernickel bread

Combine the trout and shrimp in a food processor and process until finely chopped. Add the cream cheese and process until combined. Spoon the mixture into a bowl and stir in the chives, capers and lemon zest. Season with salt and pepper. Spread on slices of pumpernickel bread and arrange on a serving platter. **SERVES 6 to 8**

FOR A DIFFERENT TWIST ON SERVING, CUT TWO ENGLISH CUCUMBERS INTO 1/2-INCH SLICES AND REMOVE A SMALL AMOUNT OF THE CENTER OF EACH SLICE WITH A MELON SCOOPER. SPOON SOME OF THE PÂTÉ ONTO EACH SLICE.

CAVIAR PIE

6 hard-cooked eggs, chopped
3 tablespoons mayonnaise
1¹/₂ cups minced onions
8 ounces cream cheese, softened
²/₃ cup sour cream
2 jars lumpfish caviar, strained
(Ronanoff preferred)

Combine the eggs and mayonnaise in a bowl and spread over the bottom of a greased 8-inch springform pan. Sprinkle with the onions. Mix the cream cheese and sour cream in a bowl until blended and spread over the prepared layers. Chill, covered, for 3 hours or longer.

Just before serving, spread the caviar over the top of the chilled layers. Run a knife around the edge of the pan to loosen and remove the side. Garnish with lemon wedges and parsley. Serve with assorted party crackers. **SERVES 12**

Baked Brie with Caramelized Onions

2 tablespoons butter
8 cups sliced onions (about 4 large)
1 tablespoon minced thyme
1 garlic clove, chopped
¼ cup dry white wine
1 teaspoon sugar
¼ cup dry white wine
Salt and pepper to taste
1 (32- to 36-ounce) 8-inch round
    French Brie cheese packed in a wooden box
2 French bread baguettes, sliced

Melt the butter in a large heavy skillet over medium-high heat and add the onions. Sauté for 6 minutes or just until tender. Stir in the thyme and garlic and reduce the heat to medium. Cook for 25 minutes or until the onions are golden brown, stirring frequently.

Add ¼ cup wine and cook for 2 minutes or until most of the liquid evaporates. Sprinkle with the sugar and sauté for 10 minutes or until the onions are soft and brown. Stir in ¼ cup wine and cook for 2 minutes longer or just until the liquid evaporates. Season with salt and pepper. Remove from the heat and let stand until cool. At this point, the mixture may be stored, covered, in the refrigerator for up to 2 days.

Unwrap the cheese, reserving the wooden box bottom. Cut away the top rind of the cheese, leaving the rind on the side and bottom intact. Arrange the cheese rind side down in the box and place the box on a baking sheet. Spread the top of the cheese with the onion mixture. Bake at 350 degrees for 20 minutes or just until the cheese begins to melt, checking occasionally. Place the cheese in the box on a platter and surround with the baguette slices. Serve immediately.
Serves 8 to 10

GRILLED BRIE WITH TOMATO AND BASIL

1 small round Brie cheese
2 cups grape tomatoes, chopped
2 cups loosely packed fresh basil, chopped
1 garlic clove, minced
3 tablespoons olive oil
Salt and pepper to taste

Slice the cheese horizontally into halves and place one cheese half cut side up on a sheet of foil. Combine the tomatoes, basil, garlic, olive oil, salt and pepper in a bowl and mix until coated. Let stand to allow the flavors to blend.

Spread the tomato mixture over the cheese half and top with the remaining half cut side down. Fold the foil over to seal. Place on a grill rack and grill over hot coals for 10 to 15 minutes or bake in a 350-degree oven for 10 to 15 minutes. Serve warm with assorted party crackers. **SERVES 4 to 6**

ARTICHOKE CHEESECAKE

1 (3-ounce) jar marinated artichokes
24 ounces cream cheese, softened
1¹/₂ cups crumbled feta cheese
2 garlic cloves, minced
1¹/₂ teaspoons chopped fresh oregano
3 eggs, beaten
¹/₄ cup chopped onion
1 teaspoon chopped pimento

Drain the artichokes, reserving 2 tablespoons of the marinade. Chop the artichokes. Combine the cream cheese, feta cheese, garlic and oregano in a mixing bowl and beat until combined. Blend in the eggs. Stir in the artichokes, reserved artichoke marinade, onion and pimento.

Spoon the mixture into a greased 9-inch springform pan. Bake, covered loosely with foil, at 325 degrees for 35 to 40 minutes or until the edge is firm and the center jiggles slightly when lightly shaken. Let cool in the pan on a wire rack. Chill, covered, for 2 to 24 hours. Serve with assorted party crackers. **SERVES 16**

BLUE CHEESE CHEESECAKE

8 ounces lean bacon
1 onion, finely chopped
29 ounces cream cheese, softened
4 eggs, beaten
1/2 cup heavy cream
8 ounces blue cheese, crumbled
2 or 3 drops of Tabasco sauce
1/3 cup fine bread crumbs
1/4 cup (1 ounce) grated Parmesan cheese

Cook the bacon in a skillet until brown and crisp. Drain, reserving 1 tablespoon of the drippings. Crumble the bacon. Sauté the onion in the reserved bacon drippings until tender. Beat the cream cheese, eggs and cream in a mixing bowl until blended. Stir in the sautéed onion, bacon, blue cheese and Tabasco sauce.

Sprinkle the bread crumbs and Parmesan cheese in a buttered 8-inch watertight springform pan. Spread the cream cheese mixture in the prepared pan. Place the springform pan in a baking pan and add enough water to the baking pan to measure several inches.

Bake at 300 degrees for 1 hour and 40 minutes. Turn off the oven and let the cake stand in the oven with the door closed for 1 hour. Remove the springform pan from the water and let the cheesecake cool in the pan on a wire rack for 2 hours. Serve with assorted party crackers. **SERVES 10 to 12**

Mexican Cheesecake

1/2 cup finely crushed tortilla chips
1/4 cup (1/2 stick) butter, melted
19 ounces cream cheese, softened
2 eggs
2 1/2 cups (10 ounces) shredded Monterey Jack cheese
1 (4-ounce) can chopped green chiles
1/4 cup finely chopped fresh cilantro
1/4 teaspoon cayenne pepper
1 cup sour cream
Additional fresh cilantro
1/2 cup chopped red, green and yellow bell peppers
1/2 cup chopped green onions
2 tablespoons chopped black olives
1 tomato, seeded and chopped

Mix the crushed chips and butter in a bowl and press the crumb mixture over the bottom of a 9-inch springform pan. Bake at 325 degrees for 15 minutes. Maintain the oven temperature.

Beat the cream cheese in a mixing bowl until light and fluffy. Add the eggs one at a time, beating well after each addition. Stir in the Monterey Jack cheese, green chiles, 1/4 cup cilantro and the cayenne pepper. Spread in the prepared pan and bake for 40 minutes. Let cool in the pan on a wire rack. Spread the sour cream over the baked layer. Chill, covered, until serving time.

Loosen the side with a knife and remove. Arrange the cheesecake on a pedestal cake plate covered with additional fresh cilantro. Sprinkle the bell peppers, green onions, olives and tomato over the top of the cheesecake. Serve with hearty chips. SERVES **10 to 12**

Pineapple Cheese Ball

16 ounces cream cheese, softened
1 (8-ounce) can crushed pineapple, drained
1 cup chopped pecans
1/4 cup finely chopped green bell pepper
2 tablespoons finely chopped onion
1 1/2 to 3 teaspoons Jane's Krazy Mixed-Up salt
1 cup chopped pecans

Mix the cream cheese in a bowl until smooth using a fork. Stir in the pineapple, 1 cup pecans, the bell pepper, onion and salt. Shape into a ball and coat with 1 cup pecans. Wrap in foil and chill for 8 to 24 hours.

Place the cheese ball on a serving plate and garnish with pineapple slices and maraschino cherries. Serve with assorted party crackers. The recipe makes one large cheese ball or two small cheese balls. **SERVES 10 to 12**

Feta Cheese with Pepper Honey

16 ounces feta cheese
2 1/2 teaspoons black peppercorns
1/3 cup honey

Pat the cheese dry with paper towels and arrange on a serving platter. Coarsely crack the peppercorns using a mortar and pestle or the bottom of a heavy skillet. Combine the cracked peppercorns and honey in a measuring cup and mix well. Pour over the cheese. Serve with assorted party crackers. **SERVES 6 to 8**

FROMAGE FORT

8 ounces assorted hard cheese pieces (leftovers)
¼ cup dry white wine
1 garlic clove
Freshly ground pepper to taste
Salt to taste

Combine the cheese, wine, garlic and pepper in a food processor. Process for 30 seconds or until the mixture is creamy but not too soft. Taste and add salt if needed.

Pack the cheese mixture in small containers. Serve chilled or spread on bread slices and broil for several minutes. Freeze for future use, if desired.
SERVES 6 to 8

THIS RECIPE IS A GREAT WAY TO USE LEFTOVER CHEESE.

CHEESE MOLD

1/2 cup (1 stick) unsalted butter
3 cups (12 ounces) shredded Cheddar cheese
2/3 cup crumbled blue cheese
1/4 cup dry white wine
2 tablespoons minced onion
2 tablespoons chili sauce
1 teaspoon Worcestershire sauce
5 tablespoons kirsch

Melt the butter in a saucepan and stir in the Cheddar cheese and blue cheese. Add the wine, onion, chili sauce and Worcestershire sauce and mix well.

Cook over low heat until smooth, stirring frequently. Stir in the liqueur. Remove from the heat and let cool for 20 minutes. Spoon into a fluted mold and chill, covered, until firm. Invert onto a serving platter and serve with bland crackers and/or toast rounds. **SERVES 6 to 8**

BLUE CHEESE MOUSSE

6 egg yolks
2 cups heavy whipping cream
1 1/2 tablespoons unflavored gelatin
1/4 cup cold water
12 ounces blue cheese
3 egg whites

Combine the egg yolks with 6 tablespoons of the whipping cream in a saucepan. Cook over low heat until creamy, whisking constantly. Soften the gelatin in the cold water in a saucepan. Simmer over very low heat until the gelatin dissolves; do not allow to boil. Add to the egg yolk mixture and mix well. Press the blue cheese through a sieve into the egg yolk mixture and mix well.

Beat the remaining whipping cream in a mixing bowl until firm peaks form. Add to the cheese mixture. Beat the egg whites in a mixing bowl until stiff peaks form. Fold the egg whites into the cheese mixture. Spoon into an oiled 6-cup mold and chill for 2 hours or longer. Invert onto a serving platter and serve with melba toast. SERVES 8 to 10

THE FLAVOR IS BEST WHEN PREPARED 1 DAY IN ADVANCE.

Poor Man's Pâté de Foie Gras

8 ounces liverwurst
3 ounces cream cheese, softened
1/3 cup light cream
1/4 cup mayonnaise
1 tablespoon Worcestershire sauce
1 tablespoon dry sherry
1/4 to 1/2 teaspoon curry powder
1/4 teaspoon salt
1/4 teaspoon pepper

Combine the liverwurst, cream cheese, cream, mayonnaise, Worcestershire sauce, sherry, curry powder, salt and pepper in a food processor and process until blended. Spoon into a bowl and chill, covered, until serving time. Serve with assorted party crackers. **SERVES 8 to 10**

CURRY STRENGTH VARIES, SO START WITH THE SMALLER AMOUNT AND TASTE BEFORE ADDING ADDITIONAL CURRY POWDER. THE CURRY FLAVOR SHOULD NOT BE DISCERNABLE.

Velvety Chicken Liver Pâté

1/4 cup (1/2 stick) butter
8 ounces chicken livers, cut into halves
1 small onion, chopped
1 small tart apple, peeled and chopped
1/2 teaspoon salt
1/8 teaspoon pepper
2 tablespoons brandy
2 tablespoons whipping cream
1/4 cup (1/2 stick) butter, softened

Melt 1/4 cup butter in a medium skillet and stir in the chicken livers. Sauté for 2 minutes. Add the onion, apple, salt and pepper and mix well. Cook over medium heat for 5 minutes or until the apple is tender. Stir in the brandy and cream.

Spoon into a food processor or blender and process for 2 to 3 minutes or until smooth. Chill, covered, for 1 hour or until cold.

Beat 1/4 cup butter in a mixing bowl until light and fluffy. Add the chicken liver mixture gradually and beat until blended. Spoon into a crock or bowl. Chill, covered, for 2 hours or longer. Serve with assorted party crackers and/or melba toast. **MAKES 2 cups**

Pâté Maison

1/2 cup raisins
1/2 cup finely chopped prunes
1/2 cup Cognac
4 ounces ham, chopped
White wine
1 pound veal cubes or
  chicken breast
1 pound pork cubes
8 ounces pork fat

2 teaspoons juniper berries
Salt and pepper to taste
Finely chopped fresh parsley to taste
Finely chopped scallions to taste
Finely chopped fresh thyme to taste
1 or 2 eggs, lightly beaten
12 ounces sliced bacon
2 bay leaves

Marinate the raisins and prunes in the brandy in a bowl for 30 minutes or longer. Sauté the ham lightly in wine in a skillet. Grind the veal, pork and pork fat together in a meat grinder. Spoon into a bowl and stir in the ham, undrained raisins, undrained prunes, juniper berries, salt, pepper, parsley, scallions and thyme. Stir in the eggs.

Line a terrine with the bacon and pack the veal mixture into the prepared terrine. Arrange the bay leaves over the top. Place the terrine in a bain-marie (water bath) and bake at 375 degrees for 1 1/2 hours. Remove from the oven and discard the bay leaves. Remove the terrine from the water bath and chill, covered, for two days. Slice and serve with grainy mustard, cornichons and French bread baguette slices. **MAKES 24 slices**

THIS RECIPE IS COURTESY OF MICHELE HAINES, CHEF/OWNER OF SPRING MILL CAFÉ IN CONSHOHOCKEN, PA.

Sun-Dried Tomato Pâté

¹/2 cup loosely packed sun-dried tomatoes
¹/4 cup small pimento-stuffed Spanish olives
2 tablespoons pine nuts
2 tablespoons extra-virgin olive oil
1 garlic clove, chopped
8 ounces cream cheese, cubed and chilled
¹/4 to ¹/2 teaspoon paprika (optional)

Combine the tomatoes, olives, pine nuts, olive oil and garlic in a food processor fitted with a metal blade. Pulse to chop and then process until finely chopped, scraping the side of the bowl as needed.

Add the cream cheese and paprika and process until smooth and creamy. Serve immediately with plain crackers, or chill in the refrigerator before serving. Freeze, if desired, for future use. Double the recipe for a large crowd.
SERVES 8 to 10

Grand Prix Beer Cheese Spread

8 ounces sharp Cheddar cheese, shredded
8 ounces deli American cheese, shredded
1¹/2 tablespoons Worcestershire sauce
2 garlic cloves, minced
¹/4 teaspoon dry mustard
Dash of red pepper or Tabasco sauce
¹/2 cup beer (Budweiser preferred)

Combine the Cheddar cheese, American cheese, Worcestershire sauce, garlic, dry mustard and red pepper in a food processor and process until blended. Add the beer gradually, processing constantly until smooth. Spoon into a crock and serve with your favorite party crackers. **SERVES 8 to 10**

Hot Beef Spread

8 ounces cream cheese, softened
2 tablespoons milk
$1/2$ cup sour cream
1 (2-ounce) package dried beef, chopped
2 tablespoons chopped green bell pepper
2 tablespoons chopped onion
$1/2$ teaspoon pepper
$1/4$ cup chopped walnuts

Mix the cream cheese with the milk in a bowl until blended. Stir in the sour cream, dried beef, bell pepper, onion and pepper.

Pat the mixture into a round baking dish and sprinkle with the walnuts. Bake at 350 degrees for 15 minutes. Serve with assorted party crackers.

Serves 6 to 8

GARLIC-FETA CHEESE SPREAD

1 garlic clove, minced
¹/₄ teaspoon salt
12 ounces cream cheese, cubed and softened
8 ounces feta cheese, crumbled
¹/₂ cup mayonnaise
¹/₄ teaspoon dried marjoram, crushed
¹/₄ teaspoon dried thyme, crushed
¹/₄ teaspoon dried basil, crushed
¹/₄ teaspoon dried dill weed, crushed

Mash the garlic with the salt in a bowl until of a paste consistency. Combine with the cream cheese, feta cheese, mayonnaise, marjoram, thyme, basil and dill weed in a food processor and process until blended.

Spoon the mixture into a crock or bowl. Chill, covered, for 2 hours or for up to 1 week. Serve with assorted party crackers. **SERVES 4 to 6**

MEDITERRANEAN SPREAD

2 (12-ounce) jars roasted red peppers,
  drained and chopped
6 ounces goat cheese, crumbled
1/2 cup pine nuts, lightly toasted
1 cup fresh basil, julienned
1/4 cup olive oil
1 cup (4 ounces) grated Parmesan cheese or
  Romano cheese

Layer the roasted peppers, goat cheese, pine nuts and basil in the order listed in a 9-inch ceramic dish or round baking dish coated with nonstick cooking spray. Drizzle with the olive oil and sprinkle with the Parmesan cheese.

Bake at 375 degrees for 10 to 15 minutes or until the cheese melts and the top is light brown. Garnish with chopped tomatoes and chopped black olives. Serve warm with slices of French bread and/or assorted party crackers. SERVES 6

MUSHROOM TAPENADE

1 pound button mushrooms, cut into quarters
3 tablespoons olive oil
1/3 cup dry red wine
2 tablespoons chopped fresh thyme
2 tablespoons chopped fresh oregano
18 pitted kalamata olives
3 garlic cloves, chopped
2 tablespoons capers
Juice of 1 lemon
1/4 cup olive oil

Sauté the mushrooms in 3 tablespoons olive oil in a 10-inch skillet over medium-high heat until the mushrooms render their liquid and start to brown. Stir in the wine, thyme and oregano. Reduce the heat to medium-low.

Simmer until most of the liquid has been reduced. Let cool slightly and spoon into a food processor. Add the olives, garlic, capers and lemon juice.

Pulse until the olives and capers are finely chopped. Add 1/4 cup olive oil, processing constantly until the mixture reaches the consistency of a fine mince. Serve with assorted party crackers, baguette slices and/or as a spread on sandwiches. **SERVES 6 to 8**

Gorgonzola and Fig Terrine

1/2 cup toasted walnuts, coarsely
  chopped
6 ounces cream cheese, softened

12 ounces Gorgonzola cheese,
  crumbled
1 jar fig preserves

Line a 4×6-inch loaf pan with foil. Sprinkle the walnuts over the bottom of the pan. Process the cream cheese and Gorgonzola cheese in a food processor until blended.

Layer 1/2 cup of the cheese mixture, one-half of the preserves and 1/2 cup of the cheese mixture in the prepared pan. Top with the remaining preserves and the remaining cheese mixture. Chill, covered, for 4 to 24 hours. Invert onto a serving platter and serve with assorted party crackers. SERVES **10 to 12**

Layered Christmas Hors d'Oeuvre

1 (3-ounce) package
  sun-dried tomatoes
8 ounces cream cheese, softened
3 tablespoons sour cream

1 green onion, chopped
1/2 tall jar fresh pesto
Freshly shaved Parmesan cheese
20 to 30 pine nuts

Combine the sun-dried tomatoes with enough water to cover in a saucepan and bring to a boil. Remove from the heat and let stand for several minutes to rehydrate. Drain and chop.

Spread the tomatoes on a round platter. Mix the cream cheese, sour cream and green onion in a bowl until combined. Spread over the tomatoes. Spread the prepared layers with the pesto and sprinkle with Parmesan cheese.

Microwave the pine nuts in a microwave-safe dish for 2 minutes. Press the pine nuts into the top. Serve at room temperature or chilled with plain crackers. SERVES **8 to 10**

MEDITERRANEAN TORTA

5 ounces goat cheese
4 ounces cream cheese, softened
1 cup chopped toasted hazelnuts
1 cup oil-pack sun-dried tomatoes
1 bunch basil, stems removed

Mix the goat cheese and cream cheese in a bowl until blended. Fold in the hazelnuts. Pat the tomatoes dry with paper towels. Mince the tomatoes with a knife or process in a food processor.

Line a 2-cup mold with plastic wrap, allowing a 2-inch overhang. Spread one-fourth of the tomatoes over the bottom of the prepared mold. Layer with one-fourth of the cheese mixture, packing down and smoothing the top with the back of a spoon. Cover with a single layer of basil leaves. Continue the layering process with the remaining tomatoes, cheese mixture and basil, ending with the cheese mixture and packing down each layer of the cheese mixture to seal. Pull the edges of the plastic wrap over the cheese. Chill for 2 hours or until firm. Invert onto a serving plate and serve with assorted party crackers and/or toasted bread slices. **SERVES 6 to 8**

HOT JEZEBEL

1 (8-ounce) block cream cheese
1 (18-ounce) jar apple jelly
1 (18-ounce) jar pineapple preserves or apricot preserves
1 (5-ounce) jar horseradish
2 tablespoons dry mustard
1 tablespoon freshly ground pepper (optional)

Place the cream cheese on a serving plate. Combine the jelly, preserves, horseradish, dry mustard and pepper in a bowl and mix well. Spoon over the cream cheese. Serve with assorted party crackers. **MAKES 5 cups**

THE JEZEBEL SAUCE CAN BE STORED, COVERED, IN THE REFRIGERATOR FOR SEVERAL MONTHS.

Russian Eggplant

3 large onions, coarsely chopped
Vegetable oil
2 garlic cloves, minced
2 green bell peppers, cut into 1/2-inch pieces
4 to 6 carrots, sliced
2 large eggplant, peeled and cut into 1-inch pieces
2 cups ketchup
1/2 cup minced parsley
Salt and freshly ground black pepper to taste
Sugar to taste
Cayenne pepper to taste
Chopped fresh dill weed to taste

Sauté the onions in oil in a large heavy saucepan until tender. Stir in the garlic and sauté until the onions are golden brown. Stir in the bell peppers and carrots and sauté until the bell peppers and carrots are light brown, adding additional oil as needed and stirring frequently. Add the eggplant and mix well.

Cook, covered, over low heat for 1 1/2 hours, stirring frequently to prevent sticking. Remove the cover and cook for 10 minutes longer. Stir in the ketchup, parsley, salt, black pepper, sugar, cayenne pepper and dill weed. Cook for 10 minutes longer. Let stand until cool. Chill, covered, in the refrigerator until serving time. Serve with assorted party crackers and/or toasts. May be frozen for future use. SERVES **10 to 12**

DIPS

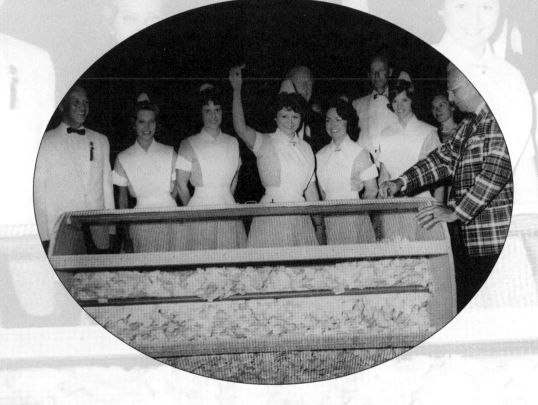

*Student nurses from Bryn Mawr Hospital draw the winning
Devon Chance at the Devon Horse Show and Country Fair.*

Five-Gaited Saddle Horses

Lee Bailey's Champagne and Applejack

Chilled Cream of Cucumber Soup

Pickled Shrimp

Cheese Spread with Crackers

Turkey Appetizer Wraps

GORGONZOLA AND CAMEMBERT FONDUE

3 large carrots, peeled
18 small red potatoes, cut into halves
18 small brussels sprouts
1 small head cauliflower, separated into florets
2 tablespoons all-purpose flour
16 ounces Camembert cheese, chilled,
*   rind removed and cheese cubed*
12 ounces Gorgonzola cheese,
*   chilled and crumbled*
1³/4 cups dry white wine
2 garlic cloves, minced
Salt and pepper to taste
1 (1¹/2-pound) loaf crusty bread,
*   cut into 1¹/2-inch cubes*

Cut the carrots lengthwise into quarters and cut the quarters into 1¹/2-inch pieces. Steam the carrots for 10 minutes, the potatoes for 12 minutes, the brussels sprouts for 10 minutes and the cauliflower for 9 minutes or until tender. Arrange the vegetables on a serving platter and tent with foil to keep warm.

Place the flour in a large bowl. Add the Camembert cheese and toss to coat. Remove to a bowl, reserving the flour. Add the Gorgonzola cheese to the reserved flour and toss to coat. Add the Gorgonzola cheese to the bowl with the Camembert cheese.

Combine the wine and garlic in a medium heavy saucepan and simmer over medium heat for 2 minutes. Reduce the heat to medium-low. Add the cheese in batches to the wine mixture and cook until melted and smooth after each addition, stirring constantly. Season with salt and pepper.

Pour into a fondue pot and set the pot over a lighted candle or canned heat. Pile the bread cubes in a basket. Serve the fondue with the bread cubes and steamed vegetables. SERVES 10

SHRIMP FONDUE

3 tablespoons all-purpose flour
2 cups milk
1 cup (4 ounces) shredded Swiss cheese
1 tablespoon Worcestershire sauce
1 teaspoon salt
1/2 teaspoon dry mustard
1/2 teaspoon paprika
1 pound cooked large shrimp,
   peeled and deveined

Whisk the flour into the milk in a saucepan until blended. Stir in the cheese, Worcestershire sauce, salt, dry mustard and paprika. Cook over medium heat until smooth, stirring frequently.

Pour into a fondue pot and set the pot over a lighted candle or canned heat. Serve with the shrimp. **SERVES 6 to 8**

BLACK BEAN DIP

2 tablespoons extra-virgin olive oil
1 garlic clove, smashed and chopped or crushed
1 small onion, chopped
1 small green bell pepper or red bell pepper, chopped
1 teaspoon ground cumin
1 minced seeded jalapeño chile, or to taste (optional)
2 (15-ounce) cans black beans, drained
Juice of 1 lime
Kosher salt to taste
2 to 3 tablespoons cold water (optional)
2 tablespoons chopped fresh cilantro (optional)

Heat the olive oil in a nonstick skillet over medium-high heat. Add the garlic, onion, bell pepper, cumin and jalapeño chile and sauté until the onion is tender. Process the sautéed vegetables, beans and lime juice in a food processor fitted with a steel blade until smooth. Taste and season with salt, if desired. Add the cold water if needed for a thinner consistency.

Pour into a bowl and sprinkle with the cilantro. Serve warm or at room temperature with tortilla chips or raw vegetables. **SERVES 6 to 8**

Black Bean and Feta Cheese Dip

1/4 cup olive oil
1/4 cup red wine vinegar
Salt and pepper to taste
1 (15-ounce) can black beans, drained and rinsed
1 (4-ounce) can sliced black olives, drained
4 ounces feta cheese, crumbled
1/2 cup drained canned corn
1/2 cup sliced green onions
3 tablespoons chopped fresh parsley
2 tablespoons fresh lemon juice

Whisk the olive oil, vinegar, salt and pepper in a bowl until blended. Combine the beans, olives, cheese, corn, green onions and parsley in a bowl and mix well. Add the vinegar mixture and toss to coat. Add the lemon juice and toss again. Serve with tortilla chips. **SERVES 4 to 6**

IF DOUBLING THE RECIPE, DOUBLE EVERY INGREDIENT EXCEPT THE LEMON JUICE.

THREE-CHEESE DIP

2 cups (8 ounces) shredded Monterey Jack cheese
2 cups (8 ounces) shredded Swiss cheese
2 cups (8 ounces) shredded extra-sharp
*   Cheddar cheese*
1 cup (or more) mayonnaise
1/2 cup grated onion

Combine the Monterey Jack cheese, Swiss cheese and Cheddar cheese in a bowl and mix well. Stir in the mayonnaise and onion. Spread in a baking dish. Bake at 350 degrees for 15 to 20 minutes or until bubbly. Serve warm with pita chips or corn chips. **SERVES 6 to 8**

CHUTNEY CHEESE DIP

8 ounces cream cheese, softened
1/4 cup chutney
1 teaspoon curry powder
1/4 teaspoon dry mustard
1/2 fresh pineapple
Toasted almonds

Combine the cream cheese, chutney, curry powder and dry mustard in a bowl and mix well. Chill, covered, for 4 hours or longer.

Scoop out the pineapple pulp, leaving approximately a 1/4- to 1/2-inch shell. Reserve the pineapple for another recipe. Spoon the chutney mixture into the pineapple shell and sprinkle with the almonds. Serve with assorted chips. **SERVES 6 to 8**

BAKED NACHO DIP

8 ounces cream cheese, softened
1 (15-ounce) can chili with or without beans
*   (Hormel preferred)*
1 bunch scallions, trimmed and finely chopped
8 ounces Cheddar cheese, shredded

Spread the cream cheese evenly over the bottom of a baking dish. Layer with the chili, scallions and cheese in the order listed. Bake at 350 degrees for 20 minutes or until the cheese melts and the dip is bubbly. Serve warm with tortilla chips. **SERVES 8 to 10**

"I KNOW WE ARE GOING TO HAVE A RECORD NIGHT IN THE GARDEN CAFÉ BASED ON HOW LONG THE HAMBURGER LINE IS . . . AND THE FRIES LINE IS . . . IF THEY ARE HALFWAY ACROSS THE WALKWAY BY 6 O'CLOCK, WE ARE GOING TO HAVE A BUSY NIGHT . . ."

—JIM ISRAEL
    CULINARY CONCEPTS

GREEN CHILE AND ARTICHOKE DIP

1 (14-ounce) can artichoke hearts,
drained and chopped
1 (4-ounce) can green chiles, rinsed,
seeded and chopped
1 cup (4 ounces) grated Parmesan cheese
1 cup mayonnaise

Combine the artichokes, green chiles and cheese in a bowl and mix well. Stir in the mayonnaise. Spread in an 8×8-inch baking dish.

Bake at 350 degrees for 20 minutes or until heated through. Serve warm with chips. **SERVES 6 to 8**

WHITE CORN DIP

8 ounces cream cheese, cubed
1/4 cup (1/2 stick) butter
1 (16-ounce) package frozen white corn, thawed
2 tablespoons milk
2 tablespoons chopped green chiles or
jalapeño chile
1/2 teaspoon garlic powder

Combine the cream cheese and butter in a saucepan. Cook over low heat until blended, stirring frequently. Stir in the corn, milk, green chiles and garlic powder. Cook until heated through.

Spoon into a heatproof serving bowl and serve warm with tortilla chips. The flavor is enhanced if prepared one day in advance and stored, covered, in the refrigerator. Reheat before serving. **SERVES 6 to 8**

LAYERED ITALIAN DIP

8 ounces cream cheese, softened
6 ounces goat cheese
2 garlic cloves, minced
8 ounces oil-pack sun-dried tomatoes,
*   drained and chopped*
6 ounces pesto

Line a small dish with plastic wrap. Mix the cream cheese and goat cheese in a bowl. Combine the garlic and tomatoes in a bowl and mix well. Spread one-third of the cheese mixture over the bottom of the prepared dish. Layer with the tomato mixture, one-half of the remaining cheese mixture, the pesto and the remaining cheese mixture. Chill, covered, for 1 hour or longer. Invert onto a serving plate and remove the plastic wrap. Serve with assorted crackers. SERVES **8 to 10**

RADISH DIP

8 ounces cream cheese, softened
1 tablespoon lemon juice
1 teaspoon salt
1 garlic clove, crushed
1/4 teaspoon dill weed
1 cup finely chopped radishes

Combine the cream cheese, lemon juice, salt, garlic and dill weed in a bowl and mix well. Add the radishes and stir until combined. Chill, covered, for 2 hours before serving. Serve with assorted chips. SERVES **4 to 6**

Spinach and Artichoke Dip

2 cups cooked spinach, drained
    and chopped
1 cup mayonnaise
1/2 cup (2 ounces) grated
    Parmesan cheese

4 ounces Swiss cheese, chopped
1 (14-ounce) can artichoke hearts,
    drained and chopped
1/2 cup (2 ounces) grated
    Parmesan cheese

Press the excess moisture from the spinach. Combine with the mayonnaise, 1/2 cup Parmesan cheese, the Swiss cheese and artichoke hearts in a bowl and mix well.

Spoon into a shallow baking dish and sprinkle with 1/2 cup Parmesan cheese. Bake at 325 degrees for 15 to 20 minutes or until brown and bubbly. Serve warm with tortilla chips. **Serves 6 to 8**

Zucchini Basil Dip

2 cups chopped zucchini
1 cup packed fresh basil leaves
1/4 cup (1 ounce) freshly grated
    Parmesan cheese
1/4 cup minced scallions
    (white and green parts)

1/4 cup minced fresh parsley
1/4 cup pine nuts, toasted
1 or 2 garlic cloves, minced
    (optional)
Salt and white pepper taste

Blanch the zucchini in a small amount of water in a saucepan for 5 minutes; drain. Press the excess moisture from the zucchini. Combine with the basil, cheese, scallions, parsley, pine nuts, garlic, salt and white pepper in a food processor fitted with a metal blade or in a blender.

Process until smooth, scraping the side of the bowl as needed. Taste and adjust the seasonings. Prepare up to 3 days in advance and store, covered, in the refrigerator. Serve with assorted chips. **Makes about 4 cups**

BLUE ROOM TACO DIP

1 (16-ounce) can refried beans
8 ounces cream cheese, softened
1 cup sour cream
Taco sauce to taste
Chopped jalapeño chiles to taste
Shredded cheese to taste
Chopped tomatoes to taste

Spread the beans over the bottom of a plate. Mix the cream cheese and sour cream in a bowl until blended and spread over the beans. Layer with taco sauce, jalapeño chiles, shredded cheese and chopped tomatoes in the order listed. Serve with tortilla chips. SERVES **6 to 8**

PREPARE IN A GLASS PIE PLATE SO THE LAYERS CAN BE SEEN.

SUN-DRIED TOMATO DIP

8 oil-pack sun-dried tomatoes,
*   drained and chopped*
8 ounces cream cheese, cubed and softened
1/2 cup sour cream
1/2 cup mayonnaise
10 dashes of Tabasco sauce
1 teaspoon coarse salt
3/4 teaspoon freshly ground pepper
2 scallions, thinly sliced
*   (white and green parts)*

Combine the tomatoes, cream cheese, sour cream, mayonnaise, Tabasco sauce, salt and pepper in a food processor and process until the tomatoes are minced. Add the scallions and pulse twice. Spoon into a serving bowl and serve at room temperature with assorted crackers and/or raw vegetables. SERVES **6 to 8**

PUMPKIN DIP

12 ounces cream cheese, softened
3/4 cup canned pumpkin
3 ounces dried beef, chopped
1 tablespoon taco seasoning
1/8 teaspoon garlic powder
1/3 cup chopped red bell pepper
1/3 cup chopped green bell pepper
1 (4-ounce) can chopped black olives

Combine the cream cheese and pumpkin in a bowl and mix until smooth. Stir in the dried beef, taco seasoning and garlic powder. Add the bell peppers and olives and mix well. Serve with assorted chips. SERVES 8 to 10

THIS IS FUN TO SERVE ON HALLOWEEN.

Reuben Dip

1 pound corned beef, shaved and chopped
1 (16-ounce) can sauerkraut, drained
8 ounces Swiss cheese, shredded
1 cup mayonnaise
2 tablespoons brown mustard

Combine the corned beef, sauerkraut, cheese, mayonnaise and brown mustard in a bowl and mix well. Spoon into a 2-quart baking dish.

Bake at 350 degrees for 30 minutes or until brown and bubbly. Serve warm with party rye bread. SERVES **6 to 8**

Taco Pie Dip

1 pound ground beef
1 (8-ounce) can tomato sauce
1 (4-ounce) can chopped green chiles
1/2 cup water
1 envelope taco seasoning mix
8 ounces cream cheese, softened
2 cups (8 ounces) shredded Monterey Jack cheese

Brown the ground beef in a skillet, stirring until crumbly; drain. Combine the tomato sauce, green chiles, water and seasoning mix in a microwave-safe bowl and mix well. Stir in the ground beef. Microwave for 5 minutes, stirring halfway through.

Spread the cream cheese over the bottom of an 8×8-inch baking dish and top with the ground beef mixture. Sprinkle with the Monterey Jack cheese. Bake at 350 degrees for 25 minutes. Serve warm with tortilla chips. SERVES **6 to 8**

ANCHOVY DIP

1 (2-ounce) can flat anchovy fillets,
*   drained and rinsed*
1/4 cup chopped parsley
1 tablespoon chopped fresh chives
2 teaspoons capers, rinsed
Pepper to taste
1 1/2 cups mayonnaise

Combine the anchovies, parsley, chives, capers and pepper in a food processor and process until smooth. Add the mayonnaise and process just until the mayonnaise is blended.

Chill, covered, for 2 hours or longer to allow the flavors to blend. Serve with crudités. **SERVES 6 to 8**

BLUE ROOM HOST'S CRAB DIP

1 package imitation crab meat
8 ounces cream cheese, softened
2 teaspoons horseradish (use Kelchner's to give his cousin the business)
2 tablespoons Worcestershire sauce
1 jar cocktail sauce (again, use Kelchner's to give his cousin business and
   because they are so good)

Rinse and flake the crab meat. Combine with the cream cheese, horseradish and Worcestershire sauce in a mixing bowl and beat until combined. Shape into a ball and wrap with plastic wrap.

Chill, covered, for 8 to 10 hours. Remove the plastic wrap and place the crab meat ball on a serving plate. Pour the cocktail sauce over the top and serve with assorted crackers. SERVES **10 to 12**

SKIP WEIDNER, A FAVORITE BLUE ROOM HOST FOR YEARS, SUBMITTED THIS RECIPE.

CREAMY CRAB MEAT DIP

7 ounces lump crab meat, drained and flaked
8 ounces cream cheese, softened
^{1}/2 cup mayonnaise
2 green onions, trimmed and chopped
Dash of Tabasco sauce or Worcestershire sauce
Slivered almonds

Combine the crab meat, cream cheese, mayonnaise, green onions and Tabasco sauce in a bowl and mix well. Spread in a decorative baking dish and sprinkle with almonds.

Bake at 350 degrees for 25 minutes or until brown and bubbly. Serve warm with assorted crackers, toast and/or rounds of fresh French bread. **SERVES 6 to 8**

HOT JALAPEÑO CRAB DIP

1 pound lump crab meat, drained and flaked
4 ounces Pepper Jack cheese, shredded
1/2 cup mayonnaise
1/2 cup chopped pickled jalapeño chiles
1 teaspoon minced garlic
1 teaspoon Worcestershire sauce
1 teaspoon Tabasco sauce
1/2 teaspoon salt
2 ounces Parmigiano-Reggiano cheese, grated

Combine the crab meat, Pepper Jack cheese, mayonnaise, jalapeño chiles, garlic, Worcestershire sauce, Tabasco sauce and salt in a bowl and mix gently. Spoon into a medium shallow baking dish and sprinkle with the Parmigiano-Reggiano cheese.

Bake at 350 degrees for 25 minutes or until brown and bubbly. Let stand for 5 minutes before serving. Serve with chips, assorted crackers, crudités and/or croutons. SERVES **8 to 10**

WARM CRAB ARTICHOKE DIP

2 ounces cream cheese, softened
1/2 cup mayonnaise
Salt and pepper to taste
4 ounces (3/4 cup) crab meat, drained
  and flaked
1/4 cup (1 ounce) grated Parmesan cheese
3 tablespoons chopped drained
  marinated artichoke hearts
2 tablespoons sliced green onions
2 tablespoon chopped red bell pepper
2 tablespoons finely chopped celery
1 1/2 tablespoons sherry wine vinegar
1 tablespoon finely chopped fresh
  Italian parsley
1/2 teaspoon Tabasco sauce
2 tablespoons grated Parmesan cheese

Beat the cream cheese in a mixing bowl until creamy. Add the mayonnaise and beat until blended. Season with salt and pepper. Fold in the crab meat, 1/4 cup Parmesan cheese, the artichokes, green onions, bell pepper, celery, vinegar, parsley and Tabasco sauce.

Spoon into a 2-cup soufflé dish and sprinkle with 2 tablespoons Parmesan cheese. Bake at 400 degrees for 15 minutes or until the cheese melts and the dip is heated through. Serve warm with toasted baguette slices and/or assorted crackers. **MAKES 1 1/2 cups**

SHRIMP DIP

4 ounces cream cheese, softened
1/3 cup sour cream
1/4 cup mayonnaise
1/2 onion, minced
2 scallions, chopped
1 1/2 tablespoons chili sauce
1 tablespoon lemon juice
1 1/2 teaspoons horseradish
1 teaspoon Worcestershire sauce
1/2 teaspoon minced garlic
2 dashes of Tabasco sauce
12 ounces cooked peeled shrimp, chopped

Beat the cream cheese, sour cream and mayonnaise in a mixing bowl until smooth. Stir in the onion, scallions, chili sauce, lemon juice, horseradish, Worcestershire sauce, garlic and Tabasco sauce. Fold in the shrimp.

Chill, covered, until serving time. Serve with chips and/or assorted crackers.
MAKES 3 1/2 cups

SAUSAGE DIP

1 pound hot bulk pork sausage
5 green onions, chopped
1 cup sour cream
1/2 cup mayonnaise
1/2 cup (2 ounces) grated Parmesan cheese
1/2 cup (2 ounces) shredded Cheddar cheese
1 (2-ounce) jar chopped pimento

Brown the sausage with the onions in a skillet, stirring until the sausage is crumbly; drain. Stir in the sour cream, mayonnaise, Parmesan cheese, Cheddar cheese and pimento.

Spoon into a baking dish. Bake at 350 degrees for 20 to 25 minutes or until brown and bubbly. Serve warm with Triscuits. **SERVES 6 to 8**

BACON DIP

8 ounces cream cheese, softened
1 cup sour cream
3 tablespoons chopped chives
1 tablespoon horseradish
Dash of garlic salt
Dash of cayenne pepper
8 slices bacon, crisp-cooked and crumbled

Combine the cream cheese and sour cream in a bowl and mix until blended. Stir in the chives, horseradish, garlic salt and cayenne pepper. Add half the bacon and mix well.

Spoon into a serving bowl and sprinkle with the remaining bacon. Serve with chips and/or assorted crackers. **SERVES 6 to 8**

SWISS AND BACON DIP

8 ounces cream cheese, softened
¹/2 cup mayonnaise
2 teaspoons (rounded) Dijon mustard
1¹/2 cups (6 ounces) shredded Swiss cheese
8 slices bacon, crisp-cooked and crumbled
3 scallions, sliced
¹/2 cup smoked almonds, coarsely chopped

Combine the cream cheese, mayonnaise and Dijon mustard in a bowl and mix until blended. Stir in the Swiss cheese, bacon and scallions. Spread in a small baking dish.

Bake at 400 degrees for 15 to 18 minutes or until bubbly around the edges. Sprinkle with the almonds. Serve warm with flat breads, baguette slices and/or baby carrots. **SERVES 6 to 8**

"DEVON IS WHERE I HAD MY FIRST KISS, MY FIRST BEER, AND MY FIRST SMOKE . . . THE ONLY THING THAT HAS CHANGED IS THAT NOW I AM WEARING A TIE."

—WADE MCDEVITT
PRESIDENT, DEVON HORSE SHOW

BLUE CHEESE DIP

8 ounces bacon, chopped
1 teaspoon minced garlic
24 ounces cream cheese, softened
4 ounces blue cheese, crumbled
1/4 cup walnuts

Cook the bacon in a skillet until almost done. Stir in the garlic and cook until the bacon is cooked through; drain. Combine with the cream cheese and blue cheese in a bowl and mix well.

Spoon into a baking dish and sprinkle with the walnuts. Bake at 350 degrees for 30 to 40 minutes or until heated through. Serve warm with chips and/or assorted crackers. Double the amount of blue cheese, if desired. **SERVES 8 to 10**

WATERMELON WITH DIP

3/4 cup lime juice
1/2 teaspoon Tabasco sauce
1/2 teaspoon salt
1 watermelon, cut into small triangles
 with rind and seeded

Mix the lime juice, Tabasco sauce and salt in a serving bowl. Dip the watermelon triangles into the sauce holding the watermelon by the rind. **SERVES 24 to 32**

Mango Cranberry Chutney

2 cups chopped fresh or frozen mangoes
1/2 cup dried sweetened cranberries
1/4 cup minced red onion
2 tablespoons water
2 tablespoons cider vinegar
1 tablespoon brown sugar
1 teaspoon ground cinnamon
1/2 teaspoon cumin

Combine the mangoes, cranberries, onion, water, vinegar, brown sugar, cinnamon and cumin in a saucepan and mix well. Simmer for 10 minutes or until thickened, stirring constantly. Serve warm with toasted pita wedges and/or cubes of black bread. **SERVES 6 to 8**

Mango Papaya Salsa

1 cup chopped peeled ripe papaya
1 cup chopped peeled ripe mango
3 plum tomatoes, chopped
1 yellow bell pepper or orange bell pepper, chopped
2 tablespoons chopped red onion,
*   rinsed in cold water*
1 small garlic clove, minced
Juice of 1 lime
2 tablespoons extra-virgin olive oil
Minced jalapeño chile or
*   serrano chile to taste*
Chopped fresh cilantro to taste
Kosher salt and freshly ground pepper to taste

Combine the papaya, mango, tomatoes, bell pepper, onion and garlic in a bowl and mix well. Stir in the lime juice, olive oil, jalapeño chile, cilantro, salt and pepper.

Taste and adjust the seasonings. Serve with tortilla chips or plantain chips, or as an accompaniment to grilled chicken, beef or fish. SERVES **10 to 12**

YOU MAY PREPARE THE SALSA UP TO 1 DAY IN ADVANCE AND STORE, COVERED, IN THE REFRIGERATOR.

SALSA DI PARMIGIANO

8 ounces Parmesan cheese, cut into 1-inch pieces
8 ounces asiago cheese, cut into 1-inch pieces
2 tablespoons chopped green onion
2 teaspoons minced garlic
2 teaspoons dried oregano
1¹/₂ cups extra-virgin olive oil
1 teaspoon freshly ground black pepper
1 teaspoon red pepper flakes

Combine the Parmesan cheese and asiago cheese in a food processor and pulse until the cheese mixture reaches the consistency of fine pea gravel. Combine with the green onion and garlic in a bowl and mix well. Add the oregano, rubbing between fingers to release the fragrance. Stir in the olive oil, black pepper and red pepper flakes.

Let stand, covered, at room temperature for 4 hours or longer. Serve with thinly sliced bread and/or assorted crackers. **SERVES 6 to 8**

Mustard Sauce

1/4 cup dry mustard (Colman's preferred)
2/3 cup water
1/4 cup sugar
1 1/2 tablespoons cornstarch
1/2 teaspoon salt
1/3 cup cider vinegar

Combine the dry mustard with a small amount of the water in a bowl and stir until blended. Let stand for several minutes. Combine the sugar, cornstarch and salt in a saucepan and mix well. Add the remaining water and stir until blended. Mix in the vinegar.

Cook over low heat until thickened, stirring frequently. Remove from the heat and let stand until cool. Stir in the dry mustard mixture. Use as a cocktail dip for Cheddar cheese, Vienna sausages, etc. **SERVES 6 to 8**

"THIS SAUCE IS SO GOOD YOU CAN DIP RUBBER ERASERS IN IT!"

—ERIC CORKHILL, M.D.

SOUPS

Looking down the road, it is very exciting to see the "inside barns"
renovated and updated to fit the modern show horse. Horses must have
been smaller back in the old days when the barns were originally built.
A lot of the original stabling was geared toward ponies and Saddlebreds.
Now we can accommodate the heavier and larger-built horses.

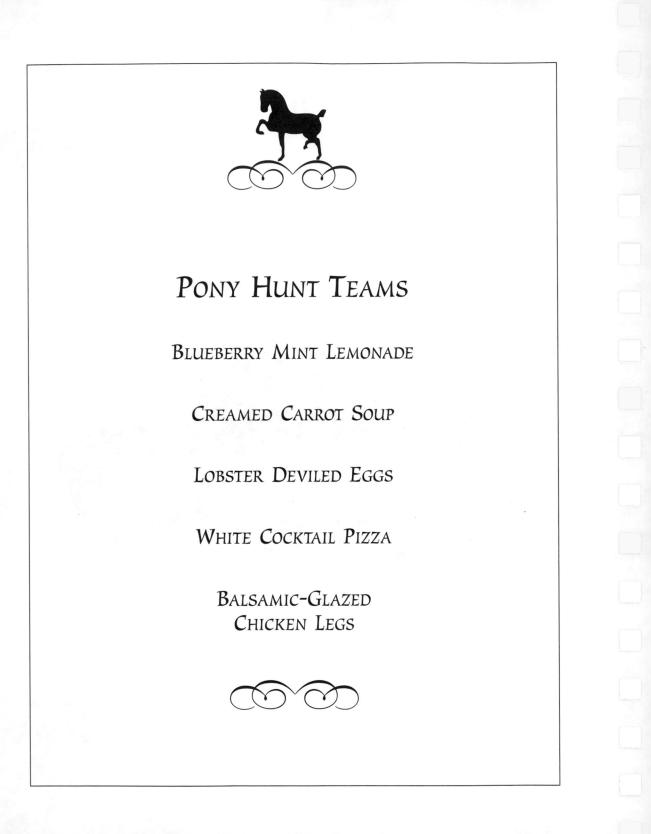

Pony Hunt Teams

Blueberry Mint Lemonade

Creamed Carrot Soup

Lobster Deviled Eggs

White Cocktail Pizza

Balsamic-Glazed
Chicken Legs

FRENCH MARKET SOUP

1 (1-pound) package dried 15-bean soup mix
16 cups water
2 pounds bulk pork sausage, sliced, cooked and drained
4 boneless skinless whole chicken breasts, chopped
1 ham bone
2 (28-ounce) cans Italian tomatoes, chopped
2 cups chopped celery
2 cups chopped onions
2 garlic cloves, minced
1 bouquet garni
Salt to taste
Tabasco sauce to taste

Sort and rinse the beans. Soak the beans using the package directions; drain. Combine with the water, sausage, chicken, ham bone, tomatoes, celery, onions, garlic and bouquet garni in a stockpot and mix well. Bring to a boil and boil gently for 3 to 4 hours or until the beans are tender, stirring and skimming the foam from the top occasionally.

Discard the bouquet garni and season with salt and Tabasco sauce. Ladle into soup bowls and serve immediately. SERVES 12

SAUSAGE TORTELLINI SOUP

12 ounces cooked smoked chicken sausage
1 large onion, cut into thin wedges
1 teaspoon minced garlic (about 2 cloves)
3 (14-ounce) cans reduced-sodium chicken broth
1 (14-ounce) can diced tomatoes with
    basil, oregano and garlic
1 cup water
2 (9-ounce) packages refrigerator cheese tortellini or
    mushroom tortellini
1 (10-ounce) package frozen baby lima beans
1/4 cup slivered fresh basil
2 tablespoons finely shredded Parmesan cheese
    (optional)

Slice the sausage lengthwise into halves and cut each half crosswise into 1-inch pieces. Heat a Dutch oven lightly coated with nonstick cooking spray over medium heat until hot. Combine the sausage, onion and garlic in the hot Dutch oven and cook until the sausage is brown and the onion is tender; drain. Stir in the broth, tomatoes and water. Bring to a boil and reduce the heat.

Simmer, covered, for 10 minutes. Stir in the pasta and lima beans and bring to a boil. Reduce the heat and simmer for 5 to 6 minutes longer or until the pasta and lima beans are tender. Ladle into soup bowls and sprinkle with the basil. Top with the cheese and serve immediately. **SERVES 8**

CORN CHOWDER

3 ounces bacon, chopped
1 large onion, chopped
2 cups chicken stock
1 cup water
1¹/₂ potatoes, chopped
1 rib celery, chopped
2 cups cream-style corn
2 cups milk
¹/₄ cup (¹/₂ stick) butter
Salt and pepper to taste

Cook the bacon in a large saucepan until light brown. Add the onion and sauté over medium heat for about 5 minutes. Stir in the stock, water, potatoes and celery.

Simmer until the potatoes are tender. Stir in the corn and simmer for 5 minutes. Add the milk and butter and simmer just until heated through. Season with salt and pepper. Ladle into soup bowls and serve immediately. SERVES 6

African Chicken and Peanut Soup

1 large red bell pepper, julienned
2 tablespoons butter
1 cup chopped onion
1 cup chopped carrots
1/2 cup chopped celery
1 tablespoon minced garlic
5 cups chicken stock
1/2 teaspoon salt
1/4 teaspoon black pepper
1/4 teaspoon crushed red pepper (optional)
3/4 cup creamy peanut butter
1 pound boneless skinless chicken breasts,
*   cut into 1/2-inch pieces*
1/3 cup sliced scallions
1/2 cup chopped roasted peanuts

Sauté the bell pepper in the butter in a saucepan over medium heat for 2 to 3 minutes. Remove the bell pepper to a bowl using a slotted spoon, reserving the pan drippings. Stir the onion, carrots, celery and garlic into the reserved pan drippings and cook over high heat for 5 to 6 minutes, stirring occasionally. Add the stock, salt, black pepper and red pepper and mix well.

Simmer, covered, for 20 minutes. Whisk in the peanut butter and stir in the chicken and sautéed bell pepper. Simmer for 3 to 5 minutes or just until the chicken is cooked through. Ladle into soup bowls and sprinkle with the scallions and peanuts. **SERVES 6 to 8**

Southwestern Chicken Soup

1 (12-ounce) jar salsa verde
1 roasted deli chicken, skinned, boned and
*   shredded (about 3 cups)*
3 cups chicken broth (homemade preferred)
1 (15-ounce) can cannellini beans,
*   drained and rinsed*
1 teaspoon ground cumin
Sour cream to taste
2 green onions, sliced
Crushed tortilla chips

Heat the salsa in a large heavy saucepan for 2 minutes. Stir in the chicken, broth, beans and cumin and bring to a boil. Reduce the heat and simmer for 10 minutes. Ladle into soup bowls and top each serving with a dollop of sour cream, the green onions and tortilla chips. SERVES **4 to 6**

"IT DOESN'T MATTER WHAT'S GOING ON OUTSIDE THOSE PALE BLUE WALLS, IT'S ALWAYS A PERFECT WORLD INSIDE THE GATES OF DEVON. THAT'S WHY I LOVE IT SO MUCH."

—CARSON KRESSLEY

MINESTRONE WITH TURKEY MEATBALLS

TURKEY MEATBALLS
1 pound ground turkey
1 egg, lightly beaten
1/4 cup quick-cooking oats
1/4 cup (1 ounce) grated
    Parmesan cheese
1/4 teaspoon dried oregano
1/4 teaspoon garlic powder

MINESTRONE
1 cup chopped onion
1 cup chopped celery

2 garlic cloves, minced
3 (14-ounce) cans chicken broth
1 (28-ounce) can tomatoes
1 (6-ounce) can tomato paste
1 cup chopped carrots
1 cup chopped peeled potato
1/2 cup fresh parsley
1 teaspoon dried basil
1 teaspoon dried thyme
1 cup tortellini
Grated Parmesan cheese to taste

To prepare the meatballs, combine the ground turkey and egg in a bowl and mix well. Stir in the oats, cheese, oregano and garlic powder. Shape into 3/4-inch balls and arrange in a single layer in a baking pan sprayed with nonstick cooking spray. Bake at 350 degrees for 20 minutes and drain.

To prepare the minestrone, sauté the onion, celery and garlic in a stockpot sprayed with nonstick cooking spray until the onion and celery are tender. Stir in the broth, tomatoes, tomato paste, carrots, potato, parsley, basil and thyme. Bring to a boil and reduce the heat.

Simmer, covered, for 30 minutes. Stir in the pasta and meatballs and simmer for 10 to 12 minutes or until the pasta is tender. Ladle into soup bowls and sprinkle with cheese. **SERVES 9**

Beach House Soup

4 slices bacon
1 cup chopped onion
1 cup chopped celery
1/2 cup chopped green bell pepper
1/2 cup chopped red bell pepper
2 cups chopped red potatoes
4 cups vegetable broth
2 cups vegetable juice cocktail
   (regular or spicy)
2 bay leaves

1 teaspoon Old Bay seasoning
1/2 teaspoon paprika
2 cups chopped tomatoes
2 cups corn kernels
1 pound fresh lump crab meat,
   drained and flaked
1/2 teaspoon freshly ground pepper
1/2 cup chopped fresh
   flat-leaf parsley

Cook the bacon in large heavy saucepan until brown and crisp. Drain, reserving the bacon drippings. Crumble the bacon. Sauté the onion, celery and bell peppers in the reserved bacon drippings for 11 minutes or until tender. Stir in the potatoes, broth, vegetable juice cocktail, bay leaves, Old Bay seasoning and paprika. Bring to a boil and reduce the heat.

Simmer for 25 minutes or until the potatoes are tender. Stir in the tomatoes and corn. Cook for 15 minutes and stir in the crab meat and bacon. Discard the bay leaves and season with the pepper. Ladle into soup bowls and sprinkle with the parsley. SERVES 13

SUBSTITUTE SHRIMP FOR THE CRAB MEAT OR USE A COMBINATION OF THE TWO FOR VARIETY.

CHESAPEAKE CITY CRAB SOUP

1 onion, minced
4 garlic cloves, minced
1/4 cup (1/2 stick) butter
1/4 cup all-purpose flour
1 tablespoon dry mustard
1/2 teaspoon salt
1/2 teaspoon black pepper
1/2 teaspoon Old Bay seasoning
Cayenne pepper to taste
1 quart (4 cups) cream
1 pound crab meat, drained and flaked
3 tablespoons sherry
Parsley to taste

Sauté the onion and garlic in the butter in a large saucepan until the onion is golden brown. Stir in the flour, dry mustard, salt, black pepper, Old Bay seasoning and cayenne pepper. Add the cream, crab meat, sherry and parsley and mix well.

Cook over low heat for 5 minutes, stirring constantly. Ladle into soup bowls and serve immediately. **SERVES 6 to 8**

CRAB GAZPACHO

1 (46-ounce) bottle or can vegetable juice cocktail
6 ripe tomatoes, chopped or puréed
2 red bell peppers, chopped or puréed
2 cucumbers, peeled and chopped or puréed
1 bunch scallion bulbs, chopped or puréed
3 garlic cloves, crushed
Chopped fresh basil to taste
Tabasco sauce to taste
Salt and pepper to taste
6 to 8 tablespoons fresh lump crab meat,
    drained and flaked

Pour the vegetable juice cocktail into a large bowl. Stir in the tomatoes with juice, bell peppers, cucumbers, scallions and garlic. Mix in the basil, Tabasco sauce, salt and pepper, tasting as needed for the desired flavor; the seasonings intensify with time. Chill, covered, until serving time. Ladle into soup bowls and top each serving with 1 tablespoon of crab meat. **SERVES 6 to 8**

PREPARE 1 DAY IN ADVANCE TO ENHANCE THE FLAVOR.

MERION GOLF CLUB OYSTER STEW

1/2 cup chopped potato
1 tablespoon finely chopped shallot
2 tablespoons butter
1 tablespoon fresh thyme
1 tablespoon chopped fresh parsley
1 tablespoon finely chopped fresh chives
1 1/2 cups heavy cream
1 tablespoon crab base or clam base
12 oysters
1/4 cup sherry
Salt and pepper to taste

Poach the potato in a small amount of water in a saucepan until cooked through; drain. Sauté the shallot in the butter in a skillet until tender and add the thyme, parsley and chives.

Combine the potato, cream, crab base and shallot mixture in a large saucepan and mix well. Simmer for 15 minutes. Stir in the oysters and sherry and simmer until the edges of the oysters begin to curl. Season with salt and pepper. Ladle into soup bowls and serve immediately. SERVES 2

SHRIMP AND CUCUMBER SOUP

¹/4 cup red wine vinegar
1 tablespoon sugar
1 teaspoon salt
2 large cucumbers, peeled, seeded and
    coarsely chopped (about 2 pounds)
1 pound small shrimp, peeled and deveined
2 tablespoons unsalted butter
¹/3 cup white vermouth
Salt and pepper to taste
1¹/2 cups chilled buttermilk
³/4 cup chopped fresh dill weed

Mix the vinegar, sugar and salt in a bowl. Add the cucumbers and toss to coat. Let stand for 35 minutes, stirring occasionally.

Rinse the shrimp and pat dry. Heat the butter in a small skillet over low heat and add the shrimp. Increase the heat and cook until the shrimp turn pink, tossing frequently. Remove the shrimp to a bowl, reserving the pan drippings. Add the vermouth to the pan drippings and boil until the mixture is reduced to a few spoonfuls. Pour over the shrimp and toss to coat. Season with salt and pepper.

Drain the cucumbers and process briefly in a food processor. Add the buttermilk and process until smooth. Add the dill weed and process for 1 second. Pour into a bowl and stir in the undrained shrimp. Chill, covered, until cold. Ladle into chilled soup bowls and garnish with additional fresh dill weed.
SERVES 4 to 6

A DELICIOUS SUMMER SOUP.

Black Bean Soup

1 onion, chopped (about 2/3 cup)
4 garlic cloves, minced
1 tablespoon ground cumin
1/2 to 1 teaspoon crushed red
    pepper flakes
2 tablespoons vegetable oil

3 (16-ounce) cans black beans
1 1/2 cups chicken broth
3 cups salsa
2 tablespoons lime juice
1/2 cup plain nonfat yogurt

Cook the onion, garlic, cumin and red pepper flakes in the oil in a 4-quart saucepan over medium heat for 3 minutes or until the onion is tender. Process in batches in a blender two cans of the beans with liquid and the broth until puréed.

Add to the onion mixture. Stir in the remaining can of undrained beans, the salsa and lime juice. Bring to a boil and reduce the heat to low. Simmer for 30 minutes, stirring occasionally. Ladle into soup bowls and top each serving with a dollop of yogurt. SERVES 10

White Bean Soup

1 large onion, chopped
1 small carrot, shredded
1 garlic clove, minced
Vegetable oil
1 small tomato, chopped

1 teaspoon dried sage
2 (15-ounce) cans Great
    Northern beans
1 (14-ounce) can chicken broth
Salt and pepper to taste

Sauté the onion, carrot and garlic in a small amount of oil in a saucepan until the onion and carrot are tender. Stir in the tomato and sage. Add the beans, broth, salt and pepper and mix well.

Bring to a boil and reduce the heat. Simmer for 5 minutes. Ladle into soup bowls and serve immediately. SERVES 4

THIS MAKES A QUICK AND EASY MEAL FOR A COLD WINTER NIGHT.

CREAM OF BROCCOLI SOUP

2 pounds broccoli, trimmed
2 tablespoons vegetable oil
6 scallions, trimmed and chopped
1 rib celery, chopped
2 tablespoons curry powder
2 tablespoons all-purpose flour
1 teaspoon cumin
5 cups chicken stock
1/2 cup heavy cream or milk
Salt and pepper to taste
1/2 cup chives, chopped

Separate the broccoli into florets. Peel and chop the stems. Heat the oil in a medium saucepan over medium heat. Stir in the scallions and celery and cook until tender. Add the curry powder, flour and cumin and cook for 1 minute, stirring constantly. Add the broccoli and stock and mix well. Bring to a boil over high heat and reduce the heat.

Simmer for 15 minutes, stirring occasionally. Process with the cream in a food processor until puréed. Season with salt and pepper. Return the purée to the saucepan and simmer just until heated through; do not boil. Ladle into soup bowls and sprinkle with the chives. Or serve chilled. **SERVES 6**

CREAMED CARROT SOUP

2 large onions, chopped
¹/4 cup (¹/2 stick) butter
6 cups chopped carrots
4 cups chicken broth
Salt to taste
1 cup heavy cream or fat-free half-and-half
1 cup milk
2 tablespoons finely chopped dill weed
¹/2 teaspoon Tabasco sauce

Sauté the onions in the butter in a large saucepan until the onions are tender. Stir in the carrots, broth and salt. Simmer for 20 minutes for a chunky consistency or 30 minutes for a smoother consistency.

Process in a food processor or blender until puréed or the desired consistency. Return the mixture to the saucepan and stir in the cream and milk. Cook just until heated through; do not boil. Stir in the dill weed and Tabasco sauce and ladle into soup bowls. Or chill, covered, in the refrigerator until serving time.
SERVES 6 to 8

CREAM OF CELERIAC SOUP

HERB BUTTER
1/2 cup (1 stick) unsalted butter, softened
2 tablespoons chopped fresh mint, chervil or parsley

SOUP
1 large celeriac, peeled and coarsely chopped (about 1 pound)
1 waxy potato, peeled and coarsely chopped
1 onion, finely chopped
6 cups chicken broth, milk or water
1 bouquet garni (1 large bunch parsley, 1 bay leaf and 5 sprigs of thyme)
3/4 cup heavy cream
Salt and pepper to taste

To prepare the herb butter, combine the butter and mint in a bowl and mix with a wooden spoon until combined. Spoon the mixture along one side of a 12×12-inch piece of waxed paper and shape the butter into a 6-inch-long cylinder using a rubber spatula. Roll in the waxed paper to enclose and twist the ends in opposing directions until the butter forms a tight cylinder. Chill in the refrigerator for up to 2 weeks. Freeze in foil for future use.

To prepare the soup, bring the celeriac, potato, onion, broth and bouquet garni to a simmer in a 4-quart saucepan. Simmer, covered, for 30 minutes or until the potato and celeriac are easily crushed against the side of the saucepan with a spoon. Discard the bouquet garni.

Strain the soup mixture through a food mill fitted with a fine disk or purée in a blender or food processor and then strain through a kitchen strainer. Return to the saucepan and stir in the cream. Cook just until heated through; do not boil. Season with salt and pepper. Ladle into soup bowls and top each serving with a slice of herb butter. For a smoother soup, strain a second time through a fine-mesh strainer after adding the cream. SERVES **6 to 8**

THIS IS A DELICATE WINTER SOUP THAT ALSO CAN BE SERVED CHILLED. THE SOUP TENDS TO THICKEN SLIGHTLY AFTER REFRIGERATION AND MIGHT REQUIRE ADDITIONAL CREAM FOR A THINNER CONSISTENCY.

GARLIC SOUP

12 garlic bulbs, separated into cloves
2 tablespoons olive oil
4 cups chicken stock (homemade preferred)
1 cup heavy cream
Salt and freshly ground white pepper to taste

Toss the garlic with the olive oil in a bowl until lightly coated. Arrange in a baking dish and cover tightly with foil. Roast at 300 degrees for 45 minutes, shaking the baking dish every 15 minutes to prevent burning. The garlic should be soft and emit a rich deep aroma at the end of the roasting process. Let stand until cool.

Process the garlic and stock in a blender until puréed. Press the purée through a fine mesh sieve into a saucepan, discarding the solids. Stir in the cream and simmer over low heat until heated through, stirring frequently. Adjust the consistency as desired with additional stock. Season with salt and white pepper. Ladle into soup bowls. **SERVES 6 to 8**

GARNISH THE SOUP WITH HARD-COOKED QUAIL EGGS AND BACON, MOREL MUSHROOMS AND CHIVES OR GRILLED SHRIMP. USE YOUR IMAGINATION AND EXPERIMENT. THIS RECIPE IS COURTESY OF ANDREW DEERY, CHEF/OWNER OF MAJOLICA RESTAURANT, PHOENIXVILLE, PA.

BAKED GARLIC AND ONION CREAM SOUP

6 large onions, cut into $^1/_2$-inch slices
2 garlic bulbs, separated into cloves
3 cups chicken broth
$1^1/_2$ teaspoons dried thyme
1 teaspoon salt
1 teaspoon ground pepper
$^1/_4$ cup ($^1/_2$ stick) butter
2 cups chicken broth
2 cups heavy cream

Arrange the onions and garlic in a shallow roasting pan. Add 3 cups broth and sprinkle with the thyme, salt and pepper. Dot with the butter.

Bake, covered with foil, at 350 degrees for $1^1/_2$ hours, stirring once or twice. Process the mixture in batches in a blender or food processor until puréed. Pour into a large saucepan and whisk in 2 cups broth and the cream. Taste and adjust the seasonings and simmer just until heated through; do not boil. Ladle into soup bowls and serve immediately. SERVES **6 to 8**

CREAM OF MUSHROOM SOUP

3 pounds assorted mushrooms, trimmed
1½ cups coarsely chopped celery
1¼ cup coarsely chopped onions
1 carrot, coarsely chopped
2 teaspoons fresh thyme
2 tablespoons butter
1 pound thinly sliced white mushrooms
4 cups chicken stock
1½ teaspoons salt
1½ teaspoons white pepper
½ cup (1 stick) unsalted butter
¾ cup all-purpose flour
4 cups half-and-half
1½ cups heavy cream

Process 3 pounds assorted mushrooms in a food processor until minced and remove to a bowl. Process the celery, onions, carrot and thyme in a food processor until minced. Sauté the celery mixture in 2 tablespoons butter in a large saucepan for 5 minutes. Stir in the minced mushrooms and the sliced mushrooms. Sauté for 5 minutes longer. Stir in the stock, salt and white pepper.

Melt ½ cup butter in a saucepan and whisk in the flour until a smooth paste forms. Whisk into the mushroom mixture and simmer for 20 minutes. Stir in the half-and-half and cream. Simmer just until heated through; do not boil. Taste and adjust the seasonings. Ladle into soup bowls and serve immediately.
SERVES 12

THIS RECIPE IS COURTESY OF JIM ISRAEL, OWNER OF CULINARY CONCEPTS.

Bermuda Onion Soup

5 small Bermuda onions, sliced
3 tablespoons butter
6 cups chicken stock
Salt to taste
6 slices French bread
3 tablespoons grated cheese

Cook the onions in the butter in a large saucepan until the onions are tender. Stir in the stock and simmer for 30 to 60 minutes or until the desired consistency. Season with salt.

Arrange one slice of bread in each of six soup bowls. Ladle the soup over the bread and sprinkle with the cheese. Serve immediately. SERVES 6

Mint Pea Soup

1 cup chicken broth
1 small onion, chopped
1 small potato, peeled and chopped
1 cup fresh or frozen peas
$1/2$ cup loosely packed mint leaves
1 garlic clove, minced
1 cup heavy cream
1 cup chicken broth
Salt and pepper to taste

Combine 1 cup broth, the onion, potato, peas, mint and garlic in a saucepan and mix well. Cook for 15 minutes or until the potato is tender.

Combine with the cream and 1 cup broth in a blender and process to the desired consistency. Return the soup to the saucepan and season with salt and pepper. Simmer just until heated through; do not boil. Ladle into soup bowls. Serve chilled, if desired. SERVES 4

CURRIED CREAM OF GREEN PEA SOUP

1 onion, finely chopped
2 tablespoons butter
1/2 head iceberg lettuce, coarsely chopped
1 tablespoon curry powder
6 cups hot water
1 chicken bouillon cube
Salt to taste
1 bunch Italian parsley, stems removed
2 cups fresh or frozen green peas, shelled
2 tablespoons butter
4 slices bread, crusts trimmed and bread cubed
6 tablespoons heavy cream
Pepper to taste

Cook the onion in 2 tablespoons butter in a saucepan for 7 to 8 minutes or until tender. Stir in the lettuce and cook for 2 to 3 minutes or until the lettuce wilts. Add the curry powder and mix well using a wooden spoon. Stir in the water and bouillon cube. Season lightly with salt and bring to a boil. Reduce the heat and simmer for 5 minutes. Stir in the parsley and peas; do not cover the saucepan and the peas will stay green. Cook until the peas are done.

Heat 2 tablespoons butter in a skillet and add the bread cubes, tossing to coat. Cook until the bread cubes are brown on all sides, shaking the skillet frequently; drain in a sieve. Place the croutons in a small bowl and cover to keep warm.

Process the pea mixture in a blender or food processor until puréed. Return the purée to the saucepan and bring just to a boil. Stir in the cream. Remove from the heat and season with salt and pepper. Ladle into soup bowls. Serve the croutons on the side. **SERVES 4 to 6**

RED PEPPER SOUP

4 large red bell peppers, thinly sliced
4 small onions, sliced
6 tablespoons butter
3 cups chicken broth
$1/2$ potato, peeled and grated
$1/2$ cup heavy cream
2 tablespoons fresh lemon juice
2 tablespoons snipped fresh dill weed
Salt and pepper to taste
8 to 10 sprigs of dill weed

Sauté the bell peppers and onions in the butter in a saucepan for 30 minutes, stirring occasionally. Stir in the broth and potato and cook for 15 minutes. Process in batches in a blender or food processor until puréed.

Combine with the cream, lemon juice, dill weed, salt and pepper in a saucepan and cook just until heated through. Ladle into soup bowls and top each serving with a sprig of dill weed. SERVES **8 to 10**

SERVE THIS VERY COLORFUL SOUP DURING THE HOLIDAYS. IT IS A GREAT APPETIZER SOUP.

BRANDIED PUMPKIN SOUP

1/2 cup finely chopped onion
1/4 cup (1/2 stick) butter
2 1/2 cups canned pumpkin
3 1/2 cups chicken broth
1/4 teaspoon ginger

1/4 teaspoon nutmeg
1 cup half-and-half
2 tablespoons brandy
Salt and white pepper to taste

Sauté the onion in the butter in a saucepan until tender. Stir in the pumpkin, broth, ginger and nutmeg. Cook until heated through, stirring occasionally. Mix in the half-and-half and brandy and simmer just until heated through. Season to taste with salt and white pepper. Ladle into soup bowls. **SERVES 6 to 8**

TOMATO SOUP ROMANOV

2 scallions, minced
2 tablespoons butter
14 1/2 ounces tomato sauce
14 1/2 ounces vegetable juice cocktail
1 teaspoon sugar
1 cup chicken stock

1 1/2 to 2 teaspoons fresh
*   thyme leaves*
Dash of pepper
3 to 4 tablespoons lemon juice
1/2 cup sour cream
1/2 teaspoon minced fresh
*   thyme leaves*

Sauté the scallions in the butter in a large saucepan until tender. Stir in the tomato sauce, vegetable juice cocktail and sugar. Cook until heated through, stirring occasionally. Stir in the stock, 1 1/2 to 2 teaspoons thyme and the pepper.

Cook until heated through. Stir in the lemon juice and remove from the heat. Mix the sour cream and 1/2 teaspoon thyme leaves in a bowl. Ladle the soup into soup bowls and top each serving with a dollop of the sour cream mixture. Serve chilled, if desired. **SERVES 6**

Tortellini Tomato Soup

3 (14-ounce) cans low-sodium
  chicken broth
9 ounces cheese tortellini or
  spinach tortellini

4 ounces chive and onion
  cream cheese
1 (15-ounce) can tomato soup
Chopped fresh basil and/or fresh
  chives to taste

Bring the broth to a boil in a large saucepan and add the pasta. Simmer for 5 minutes. Combine 1/3 cup of the hot broth with the cream cheese in a heatproof bowl and whisk until combined.

Add the cream cheese mixture and tomato soup to the pasta mixture and mix well. Simmer until heated through. Stir in the basil and/or chives and ladle into soup bowls. **Serves 4**

Butternut Squash Soup

1 large butternut squash, peeled
  and chopped
1 Vidalia onion, cut into quarters

2 or 3 (10-ounce) cans chicken broth
Salt and pepper to taste
Curry powder to taste

Combine the squash and onion in a saucepan and add enough broth to cover. Cook over medium heat for 10 to 15 minutes or until the squash is tender, stirring occasionally. Process in a food processor until puréed.

Return the purée to the saucepan and season with salt, pepper and curry powder. Cook just until heated through, adding more broth as needed for the desired consistency. Ladle into soup bowls. You may substitute one 20-ounce package pre-cut squash pieces for the whole butternut squash. **Serves 4 to 6**

CREAMY BUTTERNUT SQUASH SOUP

2 tablespoons unsalted butter
1 onion, finely chopped
1 butternut squash, peeled and
*   cut into 1-inch pieces*
6 cups vegetable stock
Pinch of nutmeg
Salt and pepper to taste
Sour cream to taste
Chopped chives to taste

Melt the butter in a large saucepan. Add the onion and cook for 8 minutes or until tender. Stir in the squash and stock and simmer until the squash is tender.

Remove the squash to a blender using a slotted spoon and process until puréed. Return the purée to the saucepan and stir in the nutmeg, salt and pepper. Simmer just until heated through. Ladle into soup bowls and top each serving with a dollop of sour cream and a sprinkling of chives. **SERVES 6 to 8**

CHILLED ROASTED CAULIFLOWER SOUP

2 heads cauliflower, trimmed
3 garlic cloves
2 shallots
2 tablespoons olive oil
6 cups chicken stock
1 teaspoon finely chopped thyme
1 bay leaf
2 cups heavy cream
Salt and freshly ground pepper to taste

Cut the cauliflower into 1-inch florets. Arrange with the garlic and shallots in a roasting pan and drizzle with the olive oil. Roast at 425 degrees for 30 to 45 minutes or until the cauliflower is tender and golden brown.

Remove the mixture to a large saucepan. Add the stock, thyme and bay leaf and simmer for 30 to 60 minutes or until the vegetables are very soft. Discard the bay leaf. Process in a blender until puréed. Pour into a bowl and mix in the cream, salt and pepper. Chill, covered, in the refrigerator. Ladle into chilled soup bowls. SERVES **6 to 8**

CHILLED CREAM OF CUCUMBER SOUP

6 large cucumbers, peeled and seeded
1 large onion, chopped
$^1/_4$ cup ($^1/_2$ stick) butter or margarine
2 (10- to 14-ounce) cans chicken broth
Salt and pepper to taste
1 cup sour cream

Combine the cucumbers and onion with the butter and a minimum amount of water in a saucepan and cook until tender. Let cool slightly.

Process in a blender until puréed. Pour into a bowl and stir in the broth, salt and pepper. Chill, covered, in the refrigerator. Mix in the sour cream and ladle into chilled soup bowls. **SERVES 4 to 6**

GAZPACHO

1 large cucumber, peeled and finely chopped
1 large tomato, chopped
1 ripe avocado, chopped
1 tablespoon wine vinegar
1 tablespoon olive oil
1 teaspoon salt
1/2 teaspoon ground thyme
1/2 teaspoon marjoram
1/2 teaspoon bouquet garni
1/2 teaspoon garlic salt
1 (11-ounce) can tomato juice
2 (5-ounce) cans vegetable juice cocktail

Combine the cucumber, tomato and avocado in a large bowl and mix gently. Stir in the vinegar, olive oil, salt, thyme, marjoram, bouquet garni and garlic salt. Mix in the tomato juice and vegetable juice cocktail. Chill, covered, for 2 to 3 hours. Ladle into chilled soup bowls or mugs. **SERVES 4 to 6**

ADD TWO CANS OF SNAPPY TOM FOR ADDITIONAL FLAVOR.

SPICY GAZPACHO

1 large tomato, peeled and seeded
1/2 small onion
1/2 cucumber
1/2 green bell pepper
1 large rib celery, cut into quarters
2 teaspoons finely chopped
    fresh parsley
1 teaspoon finely chopped
    fresh chives
1 small garlic clove, minced

2 cups vegetable juice cocktail
2 to 3 tablespoons red wine vinegar
2 tablespoons extra-virgin olive oil
1 tablespoon lemon juice
1 teaspoon sugar
1 teaspoon kosher salt
1/2 teaspoon Worcestershire sauce
1/4 teaspoon freshly ground pepper
1/4 teaspoon ground cumin
1/8 teaspoon Tabasco sauce

Process the tomato, onion, cucumber, bell pepper and celery in a food processor until finely chopped. Pour into a large container. Stir in the parsley, chives and garlic. Add the vegetable juice cocktail, vinegar, olive oil, lemon juice, sugar, salt, Worcestershire sauce, pepper, cumin and Tabasco sauce and mix well. Chill, covered, in the refrigerator.

Ladle into chilled soup bowls or mugs. Serve assorted garnishes such as chopped hard-cooked egg whites, sieved hard-cooked egg yolks, finely chopped green onions or chives, croutons, bacon bits and/or chopped avocado with the soup. SERVES 4 to 6

Watermelon Gazpacho

8 cups chopped seeded watermelon
    (reserve juices)
1 cup chopped seeded peeled cucumber
1 red bell pepper, chopped
1 yellow bell pepper, chopped
1/2 jalapeño chile, seeded and chopped
3 celery hearts, chopped
1/2 small red onion, finely chopped
1/4 cup finely chopped fresh mint
1/4 cup finely chopped fresh flat-leaf parsley
2 tablespoons plus 1 teaspoon lime juice
    (2 large limes)
3 tablespoons red wine vinegar
1/2 teaspoon kosher salt
Freshly ground pepper to taste
Salt to taste
1/4 cup crème fraîche (optional)

Process the watermelon and reserved juices in a blender or food processor until puréed. Toss the cucumber, bell peppers, jalapeño chile, celery, onion, mint, parsley, lime juice, vinegar, 1/2 teaspoon salt and pepper in a large bowl. Pour the watermelon purée over the vegetable mixture.

Chill, covered with plastic wrap, for 1 hour or until very cold. Taste and season with salt and pepper to taste. Stir in additional chopped jalapeño chile for added spice. Ladle into chilled soup bowls or mugs and top each serving with a dollop of the crème fraîche. SERVES **6 to 8**

APPLE CURRY SOUP

3 tablespoons butter
4 tart apples, peeled and chopped
1/3 cup chopped onion
2 1/2 teaspoons curry powder
1 (10-ounce) can cream of chicken soup
1 (10-ounce) can chicken broth
4 teaspoons sugar
2 teaspoons lemon juice
Dash of cayenne pepper
1 cup light cream

Melt the butter in a saucepan and stir in the apples, onion and curry powder. Cook until the onion and apples are tender. Add the soup, broth, sugar, lemon juice and cayenne pepper and mix well.

Process in a blender until smooth. Return the mixture to the saucepan and stir in the cream gradually. Cook just until heated through, stirring occasionally; do not boil. Let cool slightly and pour into a bowl. Chill, covered, in the refrigerator. Ladle into chilled soup bowls. **SERVES 5 to 6**

Mango Soup

2 ripe mangoes, peeled and chopped
1/3 cup lemon juice
4 cups vanilla yogurt

Process the mangoes in a blender or food processor until puréed. Add the lemon juice and process just until combined. Pour into a bowl and fold in the yogurt. Chill, covered, in the refrigerator. Ladle into chilled soup bowls.
SERVES 6

THIS DELIGHTFUL SOUP CAN BE SERVED AS A FIRST COURSE OR AS A LOVELY ENDING TO DINNER.

CHAMPAGNE WHITE PEACH SOUP

4 cups sliced peeled ripe peaches
   (white peaches preferred)
1 cup low-pulp orange juice
1/3 cup peach schnapps
2 tablespoons lemon juice
8 large mint leaves
3/4 cup Champagne

Process the peaches, orange juice, schnapps and lemon juice in a food processor until blended or the desired consistency. Add the mint and pulse just until combined.

Pour into a large bowl and chill, covered, for 4 hours or longer. Gently stir in the Champagne just before serving. Ladle into chilled soup bowls.
SERVES 4 to 6

CHILLED STRAWBERRY SOUP

1 pint strawberries, hulled
1 cup apple juice
1 tablespoon honey
2 teaspoons (scant) sugar
1/4 teaspoon ground cinnamon
Pinch of freshly grated nutmeg
1 cup heavy cream, chilled
1 tablespoon sherry, port or Madeira (optional)
6 tablespoons sour cream

Process the strawberries in a food processor fitted with a metal blade until puréed. Add the apple juice, honey, sugar, cinnamon and nutmeg and pulse just until blended.

Pour into a bowl and chill, covered, until serving time. Whisk in the cream and sherry just before serving. Ladle into chilled soup bowls and top each serving with a dollop of sour cream. Garnish with additional fresh strawberries. SERVES 4

Cookbook Development Committee

Chairmen

Karen Meyers　　　Gretchen Schwoebel

Committee

Ana Biddle　　　　Pam Keller

Wendy Brown　　　Mims Kerr

Susan Cadwalader　Mimi Killian

Helen Corkhill　　Renee Landan

Deb Donaldson　　Karin Maynard

Middy Dorrance　　Gail McCarthy

Robin Lang Dugan　Carol McKeirnan

Lisa Estabrook　　Jennifer Newhall

Sandy Floyd　　　Lynn Rudolph

Charlene Fullmer　Sandra Shinners

Holly Griffin　　　Beth Wright

Norma Hamm

We would like to thank the following for their support, help, and encouragement during the process of creating the cookbook.

Katherine Corkhill

Devon Courtyard Marriott

Anne and Matt Hamilton

Leonard King

Wade McDevitt

Brian Pierce, graphic designer

CONTRIBUTORS

Murfee Aceto

Kit Alderman

Marion Anderson

Ana Biddle

Carol Bowers

Rosemary Boyer

Cecelia Bristowe

Carrie Walden Brown

Wendy Brown

Byrd Bullock

Peter Wesley Burke

Susan Cadwalader

Carolyn Capaldi

Tracy Castelli

Bill Chandlee

Anne Mayer Cheezem

Sue Cheston

Hope Cohen

Chris Congdon

Buttons Corkhill

Cinda Corkhill

Eric Corkhill

Bobbi Cowley

Jennifer Delafield

Mindy Desrochers

Margie d'Esterhazy

Susan Diederich

Laura DiFrancesco

Marcia E. DiGiallorenzo

Darlene DiGorio

Deb Donaldson

Middy Dorrance

Karen Duffy

Robin Dugan

Linda Dutton

Lisa Estabrook

Jean Farnsworth

Jill Feldman

Mary Lou Fetchko

Veronica J. Finkelstein

Sandy Floyd

Patsy Forrest

Tricia Fox

Fran Franecke

Frank Gainor

Jane Gardner

Marge Glennon

Phillip Greenberg

Lois Grieshober

Holly Griffin

Candance Guinan

Norma Hamm

Mary Ellen Hankele

Ann C. Hazan

May Holgren

Dorinda Hollenbeck

Jeanne Honish

Pat Huggard

Linda Inman

Cathy Keller

Pam Keller

Susan Kent

Pamela Kerchner

Elaine Kicak

Mimi Killian

Candy Kirby

Julia Kornienko

Gail Kraungold

Evelyn Kronmiller

Irene Landon

Nancy Ligget

Tim Ligget

Leslie Little

Mary Helen Madden

Jane Malyn

Sandy Manthorpe

Molly Markle

Debbie Martin

Liz Mayer

Karin Maynard

Gail McCarthy

Graham McCleary

Wade McDevitt

Jennifer McGowan

Clary Meyers

Karen Meyers

Jennifer Mihock

Hope Miller

Karen Miller

Bob Monday

Mary Anne Morgan

Mrs. Ernest Mosley

Carmen Neilson

Sally Newbold

Joan Oates

Sally Odiorne

Irene Owens

Wendy Paul

Sandy Pew

Ann Pogyor

Lois and Bob Pogyor

Betty Riccardi

Judith Rosato

Carolyn Sanaitis

Carla and John Schaeffer

Kristen Schrader

Nancy Schriber

Peg Schwartz

Gretchen Schwoebel

Nancy Schwoebel

Ann Seidel

Woody Shuck

Dolly Somers

Mary Trabold

Tammy and Michael
Tucker

Suzy Tyson

Carol Vanchina

Ginni Vosburg

Jodi J. Warker

Mary Weber

Sandra Weckesser

Skip Weidner

Herman Winkler

Beth Wright

INDEX

Accompaniments. *See also* Sauces
Cilantro Mayonnaise, 45
Herb Butter, 229
Wasabi Mayonnaise, 57

Apple
Apple Curry Soup, 244
Hot Jezebel, 183
Wassail, 35

Artichokes
Artichoke Cheesecake, 166
Crab and Artichoke-Stuffed
Mushrooms, 119
Green Chile and Artichoke
Dip, 193
Shrimp and Artichokes, 50
Spinach and Artichoke
Dip, 195
Sun-Dried Tomatoes and
Artichokes, 76
Warm Crab Artichoke
Dip, 204

Bacon
Bacon and Cheese
Frittata, 93
Bacon and Tomato
Cups, 115
Bacon Dip, 206
Bacon-Wrapped Shrimp
with Spicy Orange
Sauce, 130
Bacon-Wrapped Water
Chestnuts, 136
Cheesy Bacon Puffs, 61
Swiss and Bacon Dip, 207

Beans
Black Bean and Feta Cheese
Dip, 190
Black Bean Dip, 189
Black Bean Soup, 226
Blue Room Taco Dip, 196
French Market Soup, 215

Sausage Tortellini Soup, 216
White Bean Soup, 226

Beef
Beef Jerky, 59
Cocktail Franks in Bourbon
Sauce, 60
Cocktail Reubens, 108
Devon Turf Club
Crostini, 104
Devon Turf Club Miniature
Burger Bites, 109
Eye-of-Round Roast with
Horseradish, 106
Fillet Tartare, 107
Hawaiian Beef Sticks, 58
Hot Beef Spread, 177
Miniature Beef Wellingtons
with Madeira Sauce, 127
Party Dogs, 110
Pumpkin Dip, 198
Reuben Dip, 199
Spiral Reuben Dijon
Bites, 140
Taco Pie Dip, 199

**Beoreg (Bed-Egg) Armenian
Appetizer,** 138

Beverages, Alcoholic
Bloody Mary, 19
Bubble Coffee, 34
Champagne Cup, 11
Chocolate Martini, 29
Cranberry Kir Royale, 26
Dark 'N Stormy, 21
Devon Blue Ribbon
Martini, 30
Devon Derby Punch, 12
Devon Julep, 26
Espresso Martini, 31
Fish House Punch, 13
French 75, 22
Ginger Gale, 23
Irish Coffee, 34

Kahlúa, 25
Latinopolitan, 27
Lee Bailey's Champagne
and Applejack, 18
Marvelous Margarita I, 27
Marvelous Margarita II, 28
Palm Beach Flirtini, 23
Peach White Wine
Sangria, 16
Pickering Punch, 14
Pineapple Greyhound, 24
Plaza Bellini, 20
Pomegranate Mojito, 32
Raspberry and Champagne
Aperitif, 18
Stone Fence, 33
Sunny Sangria, 17
Trinidad Rum Punch, 15
Union League Cocktail, 33
Wassail, 35
Watermelon Daiquiri, 21
Watermelon Margarita, 28
Watermelon Martini, 32

Beverages, Nonalcoholic
Blueberry Mint
Lemonade, 37
Ginger and Honey Tea, 36
Iced Tea, 36
Mint Zinger Punch, 14
Mock Margaritas, 38
Peach and Mint Tea, 36
Pomegranate Juice and
Lime Tea, 36
Watermelon and Basil
Tea, 36

Blue Cheese
Blue Cheese
Cheesecake, 167
Blue Cheese Dip, 208
Blue Cheese Mousse, 172
Blue Cheese Puffs, 95
Cheese Mold, 171
Deviled Cheese Balls, 62

INDEX

Brie Cheese
Baked Brie with
Caramelized
Onions, 164
Brie in Puff Pastry, 139
Brie Soufflé, 95
Grilled Brie with Tomato
and Basil, 165
Peach and Brie
Quesadillas, 133
Pecan Brie Tarts, 118
Shiitake and Brie
Pizza, 100

Canapés
Charleston Canapé, 89
Chive Bread with
Radishes, 96
Crabby Cheese Canapés, 86
Cucumber Sandwiches, 112
Curried Tuna Canapés, 91
Devon Turf Club
Delights, 94
Grilled Polenta Rounds, 98
Mango Crab Stacks, 87
Parmesan Onion Puffs, 97

Cauliflower
Chilled Roasted Cauliflower
Soup, 239
Cocktail Cauliflower, 70

Caviar Pie, 163

Cheddar Cheese
Baked Nacho Dip, 192
Cheese Mold, 171
Cheesy Bacon Puffs, 61
Crabby Cheese
Canapés, 86
Grand Prix Beer Cheese
Spread, 176
Hot Cheese and Olive
Puffs, 73
Shrimp Log, 153

Cheese. *See also* Blue Cheese;
Brie Cheese; Cheddar
Cheese; Parmesan
Cheese
Bacon and Cheese
Frittata, 93
Black Bean and Feta Cheese
Dip, 190
Chutney Cheese Dip, 191
Crabby Jack
Quesadillas, 132
Feta Cheese with Pepper
Honey, 169
Fried Mozzarella
Sticks, 65
Fromage Fort, 170
Garlic-Feta Cheese
Spread, 178
Goat Cheese and Pancetta
Tartlets, 117
Goat Cheese
Quesadilla, 132
Gorgonzola and
Camembert
Fondue, 187
Gorgonzola and Fig
Terrine, 181
Layered Italian Dip, 194
Mediterranean
Spread, 179
Mediterranean Torta, 182
Petite French Onion Phyllo
Cups, 116
Pineapple Cheese
Ball, 169
Prosciutto and Gruyère
Pinwheels, 141
Prosciutto Wraps, 129
Salsa di Parmigiano, 211
Savory Sablés, 68
Shrimp Fondue, 188
Spinach and Cheese
Bites, 77
Swiss and Bacon Dip, 207
Three-Cheese Dip, 191

Cheesecakes, Savory
Artichoke Cheesecake, 166
Blue Cheese
Cheesecake, 167
Mexican Cheesecake, 168

Chicken
African Chicken and Peanut
Soup, 218
Balsamic-Glazed Chicken
Legs, 63
French Market Soup, 215
Mahogany Chicken
Wings, 64
Roasted Chicken Salad
Bites, 111
Rumaki, 137
Sausage Tortellini
Soup, 216
Southwestern Chicken
Soup, 219
Velvety Chicken Liver
Pâté, 174

Corn
Corn Chowder, 217
White Corn Dip, 193

Crab Meat
Avalon Crab Mold, 149
Beach House Soup, 221
Blue Rooms Host's Crab
Dip, 201
Chesapeake City Crab
Soup, 222
Crab and Artichoke-Stuffed
Mushrooms, 119
Crabby Cheese Canapés, 86
Crabby Jack
Quesadillas, 132
Crab Claws with Mustard
Sauce, 41
Crab Gazpacho, 223
Crab Mousse Mold, 150
Crab Triangles, 85

INDEX

Creamy Crab Meat
 Dip, 202
Hot Jalapeño Crab
 Dip, 203
Mango Crab Stacks, 87
Mexican Seafood
 Cocktail, 47
Warm Crab Artichoke
 Dip, 204

Crostini
 Devon Turf Club
 Crostini, 104
 Roasted Bell Pepper and
 Olive Crostini, 105

Eggs
 Chutney-Stuffed Eggs, 126
 Deviled Eggs, 125
 Devilish Eggs, 126
 Lobster Deviled Eggs, 124

Figs
 Fresh Figs in a Blanket, 129
 Gorgonzola and Fig
 Terrine, 181
 Grilled Figs, 71
 Roasted Figs in Port, 70

Fish. *See also* Salmon; Trout;
 Tuna
 Anchovy Dip, 200
 Sardines and Avocado on
 Rye, 160
 Smoked Bluefish Pâté, 156

Fondues
 Gorgonzola and Camembert
 Fondue, 187
 Shrimp Fondue, 188

Fruit. *See also* Apple; Figs;
 Lemon; Mango; Orange;
 Peach; Pineapple;
 Pumpkin; Watermelon

Blueberry Mint
 Lemonade, 37
Chilled Strawberry
 Soup, 247
Devon Derby Punch, 12
Foie Gras Stuffed Dates, 115
Prosciutto Wraps, 129
Raspberry and Champagne
 Aperitif, 18

Ham
 Deviled Cheese Balls, 62
 Fresh Figs in a Blanket, 129
 Goat Cheese and Pancetta
 Tartlets, 117
 Grand Prix Prosciutto, 128
 Grilled Figs, 71
 Grilled Shrimp Spanish
 Style, 52
 Prosciutto and Gruyère
 Pinwheels, 141
 Prosciutto Wraps, 129

Jicama Appetizer, 72

Lemon
 Blueberry Mint
 Lemonade, 37
 Champagne Cup, 11
 Fish House Punch, 13
 Mint Zinger Punch, 14

Mango
 Mango Crab Stacks, 87
 Mango Cranberry
 Chutney, 209
 Mango Papaya Salsa, 210
 Mango Soup, 245

Mushrooms
 Crab and Artichoke-Stuffed
 Mushrooms, 119
 Cream of Mushroom
 Soup, 232
 Mushroom Roll-Ups, 146

Mushrooms in Garlic
 Butter, 121
Mushrooms Parmesan, 122
Mushroom Tapenade, 180
Shiitake and Brie Pizza, 100
Stuffed High-Crown
 Mushrooms, 120

Nuts. *See also* Pecans; Walnuts
 African Chicken and Peanut
 Soup, 218
 Rosemary Cashews, 79
 Spiced Almonds, 78
 Union Square Café Bar
 Nuts, 82

Olives
 Greek Olive Cups, 117
 Hot Cheese and Olive
 Puffs, 73
 Marinated Olives, 74
 Roasted Bell Pepper and
 Olive Crostini, 105
 Stuffed Olives, 75

Orange
 Bacon-Wrapped Shrimp
 with Spicy Orange
 Sauce, 130
 Champagne Cup, 11
 Mint Zinger Punch, 14
 Trinidad Rum Punch, 15

Oysters
 Baked Oysters, 88
 Bloody Mary Oysters, 43
 Merion Golf Club Oyster
 Stew, 224
 Oyster Croquettes, 44
 Smoked Oyster Roll, 152

Parmesan Cheese
 Mushrooms Parmesan, 122
 Parmesan Cheese Twists, 67
 Parmesan Onion Puffs, 97

INDEX

Parmesan Pita Crisps, 99
Parmesan Tuiles, 66

Pasta
Sausage Tortellini
Soup, 216
Tortellini Tomato
Soup, 237

Pâtés
Pâté Maison, 175
Poor Man's Pâté de Foie
Gras, 173
Smoked Bluefish Pâté, 156
Smoked Trout and Shrimp
Pâté, 162
Sun-Dried Tomato Pâté, 176
Taku Smokeries Famous
Pâté, 159
Velvety Chicken Liver
Pâté, 174

Peach
Champagne White Peach
Soup, 246
Peach and Brie
Quesadillas, 133
Peach and Mint Tea, 36
Peach White Wine
Sangria, 16

Peas
Curried Cream of Green
Pea Soup, 234
Mint Pea Soup, 233

Pecans
Glazed Pecans, 80
Pecan Brie Tarts, 118
Pineapple Cheese Ball, 169

Peppers
Bruschetta Two Ways, 103
Crab Gazpacho, 223
Grand Prix Prosciutto, 128

Greg Landis Famous
Homemade Hot
Peppers, 72
Grilled Polenta Rounds, 98
Hot Clam Pie, 151
Mango Papaya Salsa, 210
Mediterranean Spread, 179
Red Pepper Soup, 235
Roasted Bell Pepper and
Olive Crostini, 105
Russian Eggplant, 184
Seafood "Pizza," 155
Watermelon
Gazpacho, 243

Pineapple
Chutney Cheese Dip, 191
Hot Jezebel, 183
Palm Beach Flirtini, 23
Pineapple Cheese Ball, 169
Pineapple Greyhound, 24

Pizza
Pizzazz, 102
Shiitake and Brie
Pizza, 100
White Cocktail
Pizza, 101

Pork. *See also* Bacon; Ham;
Sausage
Cocktail Franks in Bourbon
Sauce, 60
Devon Turf Club
Delights, 94
Party Dogs, 110
Pâté Maison, 175
Pizza Wheels, 142
Poor Man's Pâté de Foie
Gras, 173
Scrapple Crisps, 60
Stuffed High-Crown
Mushrooms, 120
Tenderloin Tea
Sandwiches, 110

Potatoes
Baked Potato Skins, 123
Beach House Soup, 221

Pumpkin
Brandied Pumpkin
Soup, 236
Pumpkin Dip, 198

Quesadillas
Crabby Jack
Quesadillas, 132
Goat Cheese
Quesadilla, 132
Peach and Brie
Quesadillas, 133

Radish Dip, 194

Rumaki, 137

Salmon
Hot Salmon Spread, 159
Poached Salmon with Dill
Sauce, 56
Salmon Terrine, 158
Seven-Layer Salmon
Bites, 90
Smoked Salmon Cheese
Spread, 157
Taku Smokeries Famous
Pâté, 159

Salsas
Mango Papaya Salsa, 210
Salsa di Parmigiano, 211

Sauces
Buffalo Sauce, 48
Dill Sauce, 56
Dipping Sauce, 54, 131
Horseradish Sauce, 106
Jezebel Sauce, 183
Lime Honey Dipping
Sauce, 133

INDEX

Madeira Sauce, 127
Mustard Sauce, 212
Oyster Sauce, 88
Spicy Orange Sauce, 130

Sausage
French Market Soup, 215
Sausage Dip, 206
Sausage Rolls, 143
Sausage Snacks, 92

Scallops
Saucy Scallops, 47
Scallop Cakes with Cilantro
　Mayonnaise, 45
Scallops Rockefeller, 46

Seafood. *See also* Crab Meat;
　Fish; Oysters; Scallops;
　Shrimp
Blue Mussels, Pernod and
　Thyme, 42
Hot Clam Pie, 151
Lobster Deviled Eggs, 124

Shrimp
Bacon-Wrapped Shrimp
　with Spicy Orange
　Sauce, 130
Buffalo Shrimp, 48
Charleston Canapé, 89
Cinco de Mayo Shrimp
　Cocktail, 51
Grilled Shrimp Spanish
　Style, 52
Marinated Shrimp with
　Dipping Sauce, 54
Mexican Seafood
　Cocktail, 47
MPI Shrimp, 131
Pickled Shrimp, 55
Seafood "Pizza," 155
Seviche with Shrimp and
　Avocado, 49
Shrimp and Artichokes, 50

Shrimp and Cucumber
　Soup, 225
Shrimp Butter, 153
Shrimp Curry, 118
Shrimp Dip, 205
Shrimp Fondue, 188
Shrimp Log, 153
Shrimp Mold, 154
Shrimp Zucchini
　Rounds, 89
Smoked Trout and Shrimp
　Pâté, 162
Spicy Grilled Shrimp, 53

Soups, Cold
Apple Curry Soup, 244
Champagne White Peach
　Soup, 246
Chilled Cream of
　Cucumber Soup, 240
Chilled Roasted Cauliflower
　Soup, 239
Chilled Strawberry
　Soup, 247
Crab Gazpacho, 223
Gazpacho, 241
Mango Soup, 245
Shrimp and Cucumber
　Soup, 225
Spicy Gazpacho, 242
Watermelon Gazpacho, 243

Soups, Hot
African Chicken and Peanut
　Soup, 218
Baked Garlic and Onion
　Cream Soup, 231
Beach House Soup, 221
Bermuda Onion Soup, 233
Black Bean Soup, 226
Brandied Pumpkin
　Soup, 236
Butternut Squash Soup, 237
Chesapeake City Crab
　Soup, 222

Corn Chowder, 217
Creamed Carrot Soup, 228
Cream of Broccoli
　Soup, 227
Cream of Celeriac
　Soup, 229
Cream of Mushroom
　Soup, 232
Creamy Butternut Squash
　Soup, 238
Curried Cream of Green
　Pea Soup, 234
French Market Soup, 215
Garlic Soup, 230
Merion Golf Club Oyster
　Stew, 224
Minestrone with Turkey
　Meatballs, 220
Mint Pea Soup, 233
Red Pepper Soup, 235
Sausage Tortellini Soup, 216
Southwestern Chicken
　Soup, 219
Tomato Soup
　Romanov, 236
Tortellini Tomato Soup, 237
White Bean Soup, 226

Spinach
Baked Oysters, 88
Miniature Spanakopita, 134
Scallops Rockefeller, 46
Spinach and Artichoke
　Dip, 195
Spinach and Cheese
　Bites, 77

Squash
Butternut Squash
　Soup, 237
Creamy Butternut Squash
　Soup, 238
Shrimp Zucchini
　Rounds, 89
Zucchini Basil Dip, 195

Index

Stromboli, 135

Tomatoes
Bacon and Tomato
Cups, 115
Bloody Marys on
a Stick, 69
Bruschetta Two Ways, 103
Crab Gazpacho, 223
French Market Soup, 215
Gazpacho, 241
Grilled Brie with Tomato
and Basil, 165
Layered Christmas
Hors d'Oeuvre, 181
Layered Italian Dip, 194
Mango Papaya Salsa, 210
Mediterranean Torta, 182
Pizzazz, 102
Seafood "Pizza," 155
Spicy Gazpacho, 242
Sun-Dried Tomato Dip, 197
Sun-Dried Tomatoes and
Artichokes, 76
Sun-Dried Tomato Pâté, 176
Tomato Soup
Romanov, 236
Tortellini Tomato
Soup, 237

Trout
Smoked Trout and Shrimp
Pâté, 162
Smoked Trout Mousse, 161

Tuna
Curried Tuna Canapés, 91
Tuna Skewers with Wasabi
Mayonnaise, 57
Turkey
Cocktail Franks in Bourbon
Sauce, 60
Minestrone with Turkey
Meatballs, 220
Turkey Appetizer
Wraps, 144

Vegetables. *See also* Artichokes;
Beans; Corn;
Cauliflower;
Mushrooms; Olives;
Peas; Peppers; Potatoes;
Spinach; Squash;
Tomatoes
Asparagus Roll-Ups, 145
Baked Garlic and Onion
Cream Soup, 231
Bermuda Onion
Soup, 233

Chilled Cream of
Cucumber Soup, 240
Chive Bread with
Radishes, 96
Creamed Carrot Soup, 228
Cream of Broccoli
Soup, 227
Cream of Celeriac
Soup, 229
Cucumber
Sandwiches, 112
Garlic Soup, 230
Jicama Appetizer, 72
Minestrone with Turkey
Meatballs, 220
Russian Eggplant, 184

Walnuts
Candied Walnuts, 81
Herbed Walnuts, 82

Watermelon
Watermelon and Basil
Tea, 36
Watermelon Daiquiri, 21
Watermelon Gazpacho, 243
Watermelon Margarita, 28
Watermelon Martini, 32
Watermelon with Dip, 208

Ordering Information

To order additional books or for more information, please contact us at

Devon Country Fair Office
P. O. Box 925
Southeastern, PA 19399
610-525-2533
dcfair@earthlink.net
or visit our Web site at *www.thedevonhorseshow.org*